K   E 8.95

The
BARRY RICHARDS
Story

The

BARRY RICHARDS

Story

by

BARRY RICHARDS

Faber & Faber

London   Boston

First published in 1978
by Faber and Faber Limited
3 Queen Square London WC1
Printed in Great Britain by
Latimer Trend & Company Ltd Plymouth
All rights reserved

British Library Cataloguing in Publication Data

Richards, Barry
  The Barry Richards story.
  1. Richards, Barry   2. Cricket—South
  Africa—Biography
  796.358'092'4   GV915.R/

  ISBN 0-571-11187-4

I should like to thank
MARTIN TYLER
for his help in writing this book and the
enthusiasm he brought to the task.
B.A.R.

Contents

Illustrations

end of the 1970–71 season—with Ian Chappell, John Causby, Eric Freeman, Greg Chappell and Neil Dansie.

14. On my way to a hundred for Hampshire against Lancashire in the 1972 Gillette Cup. Farokh Engineer behind the stumps. (Photo: *Patrick Eagar*)

15. The happy captain with the Currie Cup—surrounded by those who made victory possible—Pat Trimborn, Bob Woolmer, Henry Fotheringham, Darryl Bestall, Vince van der Bijl (partly hidden), Aubrey Lilley and Pelham Henwood. (Photo: *The Star*, Johannesburg)

16. A coaching clinic in Soweto. South African Test players of the future? (Photo: *The Star*, Johannesburg)

17. Friend and Hampshire opening partner Gordon Greenidge. (Photo: *Patrick Eagar*)

18. Chewing gum for Gordon during a break in the slips where it was our hands which were sticky during Hampshire's championship success. (Photo: *Patrick Eagar*)

19. Hampshire's championship-winning squad 1973. Back row: Richard Lewis, Dave O'Sullivan, Mike Taylor, Tom Mottram, Bob Herman, Gordon Greenidge, Andy Murtagh, Trevor Jesty. Front row: David Turner, Peter Sainsbury, Richard Gilliat, Barry Richards, Bob Stephenson. (Photo: *Patrick Eagar*)

20. Prockie and me, old friends and rivals, Hampshire versus Gloucestershire at Bournemouth, 30 August 1973; the match which brought the championship to Hampshire. (Photo: *Patrick Eagar*)

21. A happy reunion with the 1975 Australians at Southampton —Rod Marsh, Greg Chappell and Ross Edwards. (Photo: *Patrick Eagar*)

22. I wish I had a penny for every autograph I have signed. Trevor Jesty helps me do the honours on arriving to play Surrey at the Oval. (Photo: *Patrick Eagar*)

23. Training for the future? The enjoyment of broadcasting—on this occasion for Radio Victory in Portsmouth.

24. Felled—by the Australian fast bowler Alan Hurst during the third match of the series between the South African Invitation XI and the International Wanderers in 1976. (Photo: *The Daily News*, Durban)

25. Thank you for all the applause. (Photo: *Southern Evening Echo*)

FIGURES

Foreword
by Colin Cowdrey

When Mike Procter and Barry Richards came to this country as schoolboys in 1963 I was England captain at the time and had the fun of meeting them and talking to them about cricket. Little did I think I had been confronted by two of the greatest cricketers of all time.

Barry Richards is a great batsman. There is no doubt about that. He is one of the five best batsmen I have ever seen, and the disappointment is that he has been denied an international stage upon which to exhibit his talents and demonstrate his power in the record book. Tall and upright, sturdy yet without an ounce of surplus weight, he is very powerful. Blessed with a calm, quite unshakable temperament, he has a perfect technique which stems from an ability to stand as still as a rock and play the ball later than anyone else I remember. He appears not to move at all, yet his feet twinkle. He starts every innings aiming to play straight, so straight, in fact, that he is often driving the ball back and hitting the stumps at the other end. Here is an object lesson for the schoolboy watching and learning. Once he is going there is no stopping him, hardly a flaw, for he can play every stroke and the bowler is given little encouragement. Those who bowled against him at Perth on a glorious, fast wicket will never forget the experience, for he scored three hundred on his own during the day, with hardly a false stroke.

He makes it look so easy that when he comes to fail he can give the impression that he has not been trying. This would be quite unfair and a false assumption. No one could be as good as Barry Richards without a deep sense of professional pride.

In my opinion he has been the best batsman of the seventies, with Greg Chappell not a long way behind. Geoffrey Boycott has disciplined himself and there is much of Barry Richards about his technique in defence. But Barry Richards has it all and a flair for the occasion.

M.C.C.

Chapter 1

Reflections of an Exile

Just after tea on the third day of the fourth test against Australia in 1970, I drove at Lawrie Mayne, Australia's opening bowler, with the carefree approach of a twenty-four-year-old bursting with exhilaration at a three-figure total under his name on the St George's Park scoreboard at Port Elizabeth. I felt no pang of disappointment when Ian Chappell threw the ball up in triumph as he clung on to the catch proffered by the recklessness of the shot.

Why should I? In my first series I had played my part in what was to become the greatest triumph in the history of South African cricket, a clean sweep in four matches against Australia. I had scaled the heights of my ambition, and from the top I enjoyed the atmosphere. As I acknowledged the applause from the packed audience at St George's Park I could have known no greater contentment.

Yet, when I walked out at the end of that innings, I walked out on a career as a Test batsman. Or to be more accurate Test cricket walked out on me and a number of other equally ambitious South Africans. When I first picked up a bat as a child, politics and sport were simply two subjects you read about at opposite ends of a newspaper. Their interweaving has changed the course of sport in contexts wider than that of South Africa. I am only one of many victims in a succession of debates about ends justifying means. Yet the problems of apartheid and the reaction of the rest of the cricketing world to them finally gave my love affair with cricket more problems than it could cope with. Whatever the rights and wrongs of the political argument, sadly its after-effects have turned my feelings about playing cricket for a living from delight to disillusionment.

I can't put an accurate timing on exactly when I gave up hope that the ban imposed on South Africa participating in Test cricket would be raised in time for me to reacquaint myself with the delicious feeling that I savoured during that series against Australia in 1970. It is a painful subject, because of my personal loss, and more so because of the tragedy that young athletes in South Africa are now channelling their energy and enthusiasm into other sports.

The feeling of futility has increased since I reached my thirtieth birthday in 1975, not long after the World Cup had thrilled cricket-lovers, but had saddened South Africans because of their continuing exile. I watched in 1976 the uninhibited joy of the West Indies, including my county opening partner Gordon Greenidge, exhibiting again the thrill of winning a Test rubber. Television pictures captured the elation on the faces of England's players at regaining the Ashes the following year.

I have had to envy the accolades poured upon players that I know in my heart of hearts, in all modesty, have never been as good as me. Jealousy is never an emotion to be praised, but in the case of Graeme Pollock, Mike Procter, Eddie Barlow and our immediate successors such as Clive Rice and Norman Featherstone it is surely understandable. Kerry Packer and his associates found doing business with me an extremely straightforward task; the money was only incidental to a last opportunity to play in the company of world-class cricketers again.

Deep inside, my reaction to this isolation remains one of real disappointment with only a dash of bitterness. The acrimonious feelings stem from the misconceptions in the debate which still rages between the rest of the world and the South African government. Apartheid, which I deplore, is not a manifestation of my generation or even my father's; it is a product of wrong decisions taken fifty years ago. Now it is the cornerstone of the system, and within South Africa there is genuine fear about the effects should it be abolished. But the risk has got to be taken, because either our society will slowly die in its isolation or the old order will be overthrown by the violence which is already so evident in surrounding countries.

What is so tragic is that when the 'pros' and the 'antis' declared war, they both chose cricket as their weapons. Though I am sure he has never realised it, Peter Hain, who led the successful fight to stop the 1970 South African tour to England, has disrupted the wrong sport. Cricket is the pastime of South Africans of English extraction; rugby is the sport of the Afrikaners, and it is they who keep the present government in power.

Rugby, with one or two minor exceptions, has continued uninterrupted. In 1971 the French obligingly omitted their coloured winger Bougarel from a tour to South Africa; like D'Oliveira three years earlier he was reinstated, but after a minimum of fuss the tour was played. After some perfunctory political rumblings, New Zealand's Maori players have been accepted into South Africa as token whites. There are some fanatical cricket fans among the Afrikaners, but Afrikaners generally shed few tears for the loss of cricketing ties with the rest of the world. 'The Rest of the World' happily sent players to Pretoria for a celebration rugby festival in August 1977.

When Peter Van der Merwe captained South Africa in the mid-sixties his background did attract some Afrikaner support; Hylton Ackerman, too, because you can pronounce his name 'Aachkerman' in the traditional Dutch style. Eddie Barlow has always been universally accepted because he speaks fluent Afrikaans. But for the rest our very names betray our minority backgrounds: Procter, Pollock, Irvine, Trimborn, Rice, Short, and if you look further back, McGlew, McLean, Goddard, Nourse, Melville and Mitchell. Even Denis Lindsay, a fluent speaker of Afrikaans who lives and works in an Afrikaans area, has an English name, while Vince Van der Bijl, the magnificent opening bowler for Natal who was selected for the aborted tour of Australia in 1971–72, is not the Afrikaner his name suggests. Vinnie, in fact, is one of the most English people I have met; he would fit perfectly into rural England as a country farmer. He co-owns a sports shop in Durban with the Natal wicket-keeper 'Tich' Smith. When a customer asks for any goods in Afrikaans he flies into a total panic.

So in sacrificing cricket the government in South Africa has never threatened its mandate; the Afrikaner has been placated by the regular activity at international level on the rugby pitch. The

D'Oliveira affair in 1968 was sufficiently mishandled at the English end to give some justification to the government in refusing him entry. Had he been an original selection on the tour, the outcry at any attempt to bar him would have been enormous and I am convinced that South Africa would today be a member of the International Cricket Conference.

Now, I look on the exile as being similar to having had a place in a team; once you are established in it it is hard to be left out, but once you are on the outside you have to double your output to get back. Since 1968 moderate opinion in South Africa has brought about some softening of the hard lines; but the improvements still fall short of the multiracial requirements needed to bring our cricket back into the international family. The 1976–77 season saw the first major changes and with luck this will continue sufficiently for South Africa to eventually negotiate a re-entry.

In the early days of exile one felt that South Africa was being treated like a naughty boy, that long-standing ties would overcome a difference in opinion. Even after the cancellation of the two tours, to England and Australia, for which I had been chosen, a long-term separation seemed unlikely. Gradually the optimism has been dissipated until at the present time I can see no total solution.

This inability to appreciate the severity of the split was the reason why there were very few open protests when the barriers were first dropped. Not until 1971, when two series against England had evaporated, did the players make a public demonstration of their opinions. Then at Newlands all twenty-two participants in a festival match which doubled as a trial for the Australian tour, at that time not cancelled, staged a walk-off and presented a petition declaring our belief that selection should depend on ability, not race or colour.

Our gesture had no immediate effect; there might have been more ardent protests had the players been professionals. The ban deprived us of the pride and honour of Test match cricket; not our livelihood. Such is the structure of first-class cricket in South Africa it cost many players a lot of money to participate. My comments about any aspect of cricket, from politics to tactics, are still regarded by administrators with great suspicion at home because they are 'professional' views.

Concessions with regard to multiracial cricket have always been grudgingly given by the government, sometimes because of their own bitter belief in the apartheid system, sometimes because of their political supporters. The present Prime Minister, John Vorster, and the Minister of Sport, Dr Piet Koornhof, come into the latter category. They realise what has to be done to bring the country back into international sport but they are the ham in the sandwich: on one side are the sportsmen beseeching them to hurry up and make the right moves; on the other a large part of the electorate, who see such moves as the first step to destroying South African society as they know it.

Though political progress has been made, the pace of the change has been too slow to rebuild the careers of my contemporaries and myself. Sometimes the non-white authorities have hardly helped the drive towards multiracial competition by their own attitudes. In Natal, for example, where in common with other provinces non-white teams were permitted to join the white leagues in the 1976–77 season, there was a total fiasco.

The introduction of the teams with Indian and Coloured players had been arranged at short notice at the very start of the league season; the usual BP knockout competition had begun several weeks earlier. The new sides happily competed in the first two league matches before it became apparent that they had not been included in the 60-over tournament, which had now reached its second or third round. The non-whites totally rejected the suggestion that they ran their own knockout cup with the winners playing the successful white team. Instead they expected all the games that had been previously played to be declared void and a totally new competition to start. When that demand was quite reasonably rejected, the non-white clubs pulled out of the league.

Of course such oversensitivity is understandable, particularly in the light of certain remarkable dictates from the South African Cricket Association. Every cricketer in the country, for example, was excited by the news in 1975 that a team called South African Blacks would be entering the South African Gillette Cup—until the conditions of entry were clarified. The Blacks would be drawn only against the Currie Cup champions, who happened to be Natal, and even if they somehow overcame those enormous odds to win, they would not be allowed to take part in the next round. If this policy of one step forward followed smartly by three steps back had not been so tragic, it would have been laughable.

Fortunately the organisers of the Datsun double-wicket competition, Lee Irvine and Robin Binckes, had no such inhibitions. Equally fortunately they also had the patience to endure a lack of co-operation from one of the two organisations controlling non-white cricket at the time. Mr Hassan Howa, the chairman of SACBOC, the governing body of cricketers of Indian and Cape Coloured descent, refused to allow any of his players to participate, including Basil D'Oliveira, who would have teamed up with Tony Greig. The Boards of Control in Pakistan and the West Indies refused to authorise the presence of Intikhab Alam, Mushtaq Mohammed and Gary Sobers.

But the other non-white organisation, the South African Cricket Board, had no such reservations, and in September 1973 I was proud to take part in the first major sporting confrontation between black and white players in South Africa. It is worth emphasising at this point that now there is only one body, the South African Cricket Union, under the presidency of an Indian, Mr Rashid Varachia, which controls *all* cricket in the country—though Hassan Howa in 1977 continued to lead a splinter group of old SACBOC hardliners against the new moves.

In that innovatory double-wicket competition the South African Africans were represented by Edward Habane, then seventeen and later a team-mate of Ali Bacher at the Balfour Guild club, and Edmund Ntikinca. Between them they bowled out the experienced Kiwi pair, Bev Congdon and Bruce Taylor, for 6 runs, and in so doing created the upset of the tournament. However, against two bowlers with plenty of Test wickets, gaining even 7 runs was a problem. For two overs they concentrated on survival before Ntikinca decided that the time had come for heroics; to Bruce Taylor's next ball he wound himself into an almighty hoik and the ball disappeared into a wildly cheering crowd for six. Edmund was so thrilled to see his picture on the front page of the next day's paper that he woke Tony Greig at six o'clock to show it to him!

The same year Younis Ahmed, Surrey's Pakistani Test player, and John Shepherd, Kent's West Indian all-rounder, toured the country as members of the Derrick Robins side. Shepherd would later be a key figure in another breakthrough when he played for Rhodesia in a Gillette Cup match in South Africa. Future Robins XIs would include matches against non-white South African sides on their itinerary. A condition of the International Wanderers' mini-Tests in 1975–76 was that the South African side must be multiracial.

Ali Bacher, who has worked incessantly for the cause of bringing South Africa back into cricket, came out of retirement to play for a black team in the new Transvaal Mixed Leagues; so too did Dennis Gamsy and Colin Wesley, both former Test players. In September 1977, David Dyer, the Transvaal captain, and his Currie Cup team-mates Peter de Vaal (who was chosen to tour Australia in 1971–72) and David van der Knaap all joined Kohinoor, a black club in Johannesburg. There has also been considerable progress in desegregating crowds attending matches.

Each new development has closed the gap between South Africa and the rest of the world, but bridge-building over such a vast chasm is a slow process. One stumbling-block is the poor standards in non-white cricket. What South Africa desperately needs is another Basil D'Oliveira; not to go overseas but to become a hero in his own land and to play the multiracial cricket that was denied to Basil in his prime. Duncan Stamper may develop into such a performer; his growth from being just a natural cricketer into a thinking player has been remarkable for one who never had the advantages of coaching in his formative years.

Like all the South Africans who were playing Test cricket when the ban was imposed, I have tried to help in all these changes in the sporting lifestyle of my country. However, I think our greatest contribution has been in supporting first-class cricket in South Africa during the seventies. As professional players it would have been easier to concentrate on the English season or to fill the gap between them with the well-paid sunshine of Australian grade cricket.

It saddens me that in my case this regular commitment to Currie Cup cricket—five years since the ban with three as captain —should pass with little appreciation. When I asked for my release from a contract so that I could join the Midland-Guildford club in Perth for the 1976–77 season, no one made any effort to persuade me to stay. No Natal official even had the courtesy to drop me a note thanking me for my service, even though in my three years as captain we had won two Currie Cups and the Gillette Cup.

Though I am not so obtuse that I cannot understand their reaction, I still found their philosophy of 'good riddance' extremely hurtful. When it comes to tact and subtlety I have usually attained the sophistication of a steamroller; when it comes to speaking my mind, I have often allowed my beliefs to run ahead of prudence. With no history of professionals in the domestic game, my concern with the security of my future has been interpreted as money-grubbing. Though Mike Procter and Eddie Barlow also depended on cricket for their livelihood, they somehow conducted their negotiating with better public relations than I could muster.

I have never appeared on television at home, because when I was first invited I asked 'how much?' Perhaps I should have consented to the interview for the 'honour'—which was all that they offered—but elsewhere in the world payment is customary. I will probably live to regret an error of judgement, because I would dearly love to retire from the playing arena to the commentary box, and one of the reasons I played in Perth was the opportunity to work on radio and television. In England in 1977, I played journalist for a Perth radio station with a telephone report on my impressions of each day's play in the Test series against Australia.

On account of this notoriety, most South Africans would have expected me to sign for Kerry Packer, but the authorities would have been shocked at the 'defection' of Procter, Barlow, Pollock and Hobson. They have always kept their professional hardness to themselves. I have worn mine on my sleeve.

Perhaps the sense of deprivation has bitten deeper into me than I realise. As I have delved into the lockers of my memory to tell this story, one paradox has stood out. In 1967 no young man could have loved cricket more than B. A. Richards; ten years later there could be no more disenchanted player in the first-class game, with only the hope of a 'pirate' circus to breath life into the dying enthusiasm.

At that time I had spent eight years as Barry Richards, Natal and Hampshire: sixteen first-class seasons without a break, but more important, without any challenge beyond that of scoring enough runs to justify the contracts I had signed. Without international cricket, all I had left were personal targets: the most runs in a Currie Cup series, to top the Hampshire averages and so on. For some time I did burn a candle for a hundred hundreds, but even that died when I realised that it only meant an entry on another page in Wisden. I might have sustained that ambition if I could have topped the list, but the 197 centuries of Jack Hobbs were too distant to chase.

In the end this inability to cope with targets has become a weakness. I could not block my way to a hundred in the manner of Geoff Boycott; he's obviously a great batsman, though not the sort of player I would drive to London to watch. Grinding out runs is good for the England side, but I just would not be able to stand up for that amount of time. If I had been born a Yorkshire-man I would have been that much better a player; there's no question that I would have my hundred hundreds by now.

In England the *Daily Telegraph* always publishes the top twenty players in the averages at the end of each round of county games. For much of my career I used to worry if I was not in the top ten; Richard Gilliat, my county captain, used to gee me up if there were four or five overseas players above me, and I did respond. Now I don't even buy the paper any more, and Wisden, my childhood bible, seems as interesting reading as a telephone directory.

I suppose it is just the dreadful feeling that for seven years I have been marking time. In any job there has to be the lure of promotion, but I have had no incentive in a situation where I can do nothing to improve my prospects. Another thousand runs in the Currie Cup just puts my name in another cricket annual. If you fail, you are never forgiven. Your performances are always judged by the standards you have set; but for me to average 40 means enduring comments about a 'bad season'.

Even if a miracle happened and South Africa were accepted back into the fold tomorrow, I would hardly be ready for a return. Over the years in the wilderness my fitness has gradually declined, so that I would like six months to get back into shape. Oddly I trained more for my six months in Perth, where I played no first-class cricket, than for many years. There, away from the profes-sional dressing-room, I could totally relax and enjoy the help I could give to a group of real enthusiasts.

As I write, with the High Court ruling still undecided, I don't know whether I am still eligible to play for South Africa. When the TCCB tried to ban us I did not speak out in favour of lifting that barrier, even though we five South Africans had a very strong case since we have no Test cricket as an alternative. At the time, I saw the ban as a mercy-killing to my county career, though I shall always be grateful to Hampshire for allowing me to play in England.

When I think that cricket lovers like my father have never seen Gary Sobers play in their country, the sense of deprivation is enormous. When I think of the time that has passed since that last Test in Port Elizabeth, those feelings are only heightened. But I can take consolation, unlike those who have come after me, that I do have the memories of that last year in the spotlight. And my family who nurtured the ambition saw it, however briefly, fulfilled.

Chapter 2

Grandpa and Others

From Perth to Portsmouth, from Kingsmead to Canterbury, every single time an innings of mine is ended my mind is jolted back to my childhood. Or more specifically back to Grandpa.

There is no novelty in being a sports-crazy ten-year-old with a doting grandfather. In Durban in the fifties, it was Percy, my mother's father. Unaware of my parents' deliberate efforts not to spoil me, the only child, or of my father's career problems, I grew very close to Grandpa.

Neither Percy nor my own father had any background in cricket. Both encouraged rather than coached me, Percy the more so because he had the time to spare. In my young eyes he became someone special, so when I scored my first half-century for the school under-13 team—I was probably just ten years old at the time—it seemed the natural reaction to run off the field at the end of my innings into Grandpa's arms.

I'll never forget that day. It's my one crystal-clear memory of childhood. We played at Penzance Road School, a ground with a road running down one side. I was batting with a chap called Vine who was the hugest schoolboy I have ever seen; I was probably as tall as his pads. And I was sporting my school cap for the first time. When I passed 50 the captain declared, and I duly rushed off to Grandpa exuding self-satisfaction and expecting nothing but the most lavish praise.

Instead I received the biggest telling-off I had ever experienced. He sailed straight into me—for rudeness in not raising my bat and touching my cap to acknowledge the applause of the handful of onlookers. Of course I burst into floods of tears, but the point was

27

made. To this day, every time I walk out you will see me touch my cap; for a second or two I'm reminded of a much loved mentor.

Percy and his wife came from England; so too did my father's parents, who both died when he was very young. My parents were both Durban-born, so when I was born on July 21st 1945 in Durban, I was second generation South African. From a very early age I was made aware of the twin white backgrounds, English and Afrikaans; from the start at school, as an English speaker, I took Afrikaans as my second language; for the Afrikaners it was vice versa.

We lived in a modest apartment in a block of flats—23 Davdon Court. The address I can remember, but very little else about an upbringing which must have been deeply contented. Only much later could I assess the difficulties for my parents caused by father's redundancy in his late thirties. Regular meals, sunshine and cricket in the summer and rugby in the winter were my prime concern— especially the regular meals, because at about thirteen or fourteen I was only 5 ft 3 in tall but weighed around 140 lb, a real roly-poly.

My father had worked for a long time for an optical firm which at that time was run by my Uncle Brian. He had built his career on an ability to sell, and after travelling up and down country he had been promoted to sales manager. It was just what he wanted, a steady base in Durban. But within a few months big business came to the optical firm. A takeover bid was accepted and the old man was given the choice of the devil or the deep blue sea; either back on the road or out! He opted out, and at thirty-seven had to take an inferior position with the Durban municipality. With the food always on the table, the trauma of the situation totally escaped me. But the influence remained significant. The whole experience left my father very bitter. He had put in years of hard graft to achieve that upgrading, and then somebody just came along and took it all away from him. Rightly or wrongly he passed on to me a very simply philosophy: you have to take care of yourself because no one else will.

The mistakes I made in later life I am sure my Dad would have made as well. I put it that way because I am not making excuses for actions for which I was entirely responsible. But he taught me to be self-protective. For example, I leapt in like a runaway buffalo when in 1968 I discovered that Mike Procter was earning £700 a year more from Gloucestershire than I was receiving from Hampshire. My reaction to feeling wronged was to charge the Hampshire Committee head-on, the type of unthinking approach which on several occasions landed me with the tag of being a mercenary.

But in my Durban childhood I remained unscarred at the time of this great stress for my parents. Grandpa continued to have a greater influence on my early sporting days with encouragement to be competitive, but also extremely fair.

I began my education at Kenmore Primary School in the city, but though the pattern for all my friends was to progress to Clifton Preparatory School I was sent away to boarding school. Treverton School was up by the Mooi River, some hundred miles away from Durban and for a ten-year-old a million miles from friends and happiness. I hated it.

I tried everything I knew to change my parents' plans for my life—awful letters home about every aspect of the place from food to toilet facilities. Everything, that is, but actually running away, which seemed rather cowardly and, geographically, totally impractical. But one very grey cloud revealed a silver lining. I was stricken with appendicitis, and neither the school nor the immediate surrounds possessed a well-equipped medical centre. The nearest hospital, at Escort, was fourteen miles away, so the headmaster stretched me out in the back of a truck, which did little for the pain, and drove me there.

My appendix was removed that night, and when I came round the doctor had left the offending object in a small phial by my bedside. It gave me an opportunity not to be missed. As soon as I was back at school my parents came to check on my condition. I awaited my moment, when they had been joined by Mr Binns, the headmaster, at my bedside. Then, like a magician at the end of his final trick, I produced this small bottle saying: 'There you are, Mum, I told you that they had little black things in their potatoes.'

I don't ever remember my mother being more embarassed, but perhaps a seed of doubt was sown. At the end of the year I left and caught up with my friends at Clifton. Funnily enough I discovered much later that Mike Procter had spent a year at the same boarding school; it could have been at the same time, though we have never worked it out. As I moved on to Clifton, he soon found himself back in Durban at Highbury Preparatory School.

As you might expect, Prockie's appearances in this saga will be plentiful. We have played cricket together or against each other for twenty years; Clifton versus Highbury, Durban High School against Hilton College; Natal versus Rhodesia; Hampshire against Gloucestershire; team-mates for Natal Schools, South African Schools, Gloucestershire 2nd XI, Natal, The Rest of The World and of course for South Africa.

A scorecard in my scrapbook confirms that our first meeting at the wicket was in a prep school match, but I don't remember it at all. I do have an image of him taking the field for Hilton against Durban High School when he was fourteen. They used to breed them big at Hilton, many of the boys sons of farmers with muscles beyond their age from chores around the home. Ten of the side stepped right off this production line, schoolboy colossi, at the back of the team as they came out to field followed the smallest lad on either side, dwarfed by his wicket-keeping pads. This angelic-looking blond who looked as though he should have been playing for the under-8s was to become a batsman of the stature to score six successive first-class centuries and a bowler whose pace would compare with any in the world.

At fourteen he kept wicket; the following year he bowled off-spinners at us; then because Hilton had no opening bowler, he took up fast bowling. Even then he used his strange action which over the years has consistently and incorrectly been referred to as 'bowling off the wrong foot', which is technically impossible. In Prockie's case his left foot comes down later than that of an orthodox bowler.

To keep me at Clifton, where the high quality of the education was matched by the scale of fees, meant a period of considerable sacrifice for my parents. Again my appreciation of this material-ised much later, though I must have sensed enough at the time to drop very large hints only in the direction of Grandpa when I wanted expensive extra items of cricket equipment. If this res-ponse was rarely immediate it was always positive; in the end the new bat or pair of gloves usually appeared. I wanted for nothing in this respect, and it was at Clifton that my cricket really kicked on.

Again the scrapbook, religiously kept by my mother, brings

1958

CLIFTON CRICKET CLUB V HIGHBURY C. CLUB

HOME CLUB

1st INNINGS OF CLIFTON PLAYED AT HILL CREST ON 5th NOV. 1958

VISITORS

	BATSMEN	TIME IN	OUT	RUNS SCORED	SCORING RATE 50 100 150	HOW OUT	BOWLER	TOTAL
1	BICKERTON			1·2·||		Bowled	Clifton	3
2	EASTON			1·||		ct Procter	Baldwin	1
3	DAVIS			2·1·||		Stumped	Erwin	3
4	RICHARDS			4·1·1·4·2·4·2·2·1·4·2·1·4·3·4·4·1·1·1·1·2·1·1		Bowled	Erwin	60
5	TAYLOR			1·4·4·||		ct Clifton	Baldwin	3
6	PRICE			1·1·4·1·||		ct Mannie	Erwin	4
7	SEYMOUR			·||		Bowled	Erwin	0
8	SHAW			1·1·1·||		Stumped	Erwin	3
9	CURWEN							
10	CHELLEW			1·||		Bowled	Baldwin	1
11	CAVE			·||		ct Whitely	Baldwin	0

EXTRAS 5

TOTAL 83

FOR 11 WKTS.

RESULT

Fig. 1. In good form for Clifton at the age of twelve.

some outline to the haze. On October 25th 1956, as a very proud eleven-year-old, I was selected to represent Durban Schools under-14 to play the North Coast Schools; the selectors also chose a very experienced twelve-and-a-half-year-old—experienced, that is, in my eyes—Lee Irvine, in whose footsteps I was to follow all the way into the Test side. The match was played at Maidstone; we won by 23 runs.

Though I was really only conscious of my father's interest in my cricket when I grew older, he did participate in one of the high spots of the school calendar; the fathers versus sons match. It was not just a confrontation that we all looked forward to because you could whack a parent's prized off-spinner to the fence or savour the glee of penetrating an out-of-practice forward defensive shot, though everyone relished that opportunity. The location provided the real thrill. Every year the fathers met the sons on the Kingsmead Test match ground. I'm sure every youngster felt as I did, walking out to bat in the famous stadium; I imagined cheering thousands instead of the handful of relatives in the stands; I was always Roy McLean striding out to win a Test Match for South Africa. It whetted the appetite.

The scrapbook again recalls what must have been my first century, 102 retired for Clifton (Durban) against Clifton (Nottingham Road)—and I didn't make the top score; Brian Anderson made 109 retired, but the next highest individual was 8 not out. Brian used to bowl little leg-breaks as well; that year I kept wicket and he would earn me three or four stumpings a game. I remember he came from an extremely rich background; later on he lived in England for a while and then the United States, but it's been years since I last saw him. Nor have I ever seen since a Nottingham Road master, a Mr Daniels, whose kindness in coming up, shaking my hand and saying 'Well played' always stuck in my memory. Conversations with opposition masters normally consisted only of shouts at you if you misbehaved.

I still visit Neil Fox, who was my first coach at Clifton. He was Irish, and his origins lay more in hurling and Gaelic football than in cricket. But he was just super-keen, and that was more than half the battle. His sheer enthusiasm was as contagious as a dose of the flu, and much more beneficial. In the same season I reached three figures against Nottingham Road, and I made 64 not out of

98 for 8 against South Coast Schools at Warner Beach and 99
versus Durban Prep School.

Very pleased I was, quite naturally, with such successes. Coping
with failure provided more serious problems—like hours of
sobbing when I made the long trip back for o in an early representative game after spending half the previous night ensuring my kit
was in immaculate condition for the grand occasion. I managed to
beat the problem of failure equalling tears soon enough, but I was
an established county cricketer in England before I was able to
come to terms completely with a run of low scores.

None of these early triumphs at Clifton arrived by any divine
intervention. I practised religiously; more hours in the nets meant
greater rewards, which in turn encouraged further practice. My
mother could hardly drag me indoors from a disused tennis court
alongside Davdon Court. Three brothers, Keith, Brian and
Rodney Morris, who lived opposite, were my partners and
opponents; we embarked on enormous contests that stretched
through many a summer afternoon and evening. I was the
youngest, so I suppose I had the toughest upbringing as we lived
out our dreams with a cut-down bat to cope with underarm
bowling propelled with as much speed as our growing bodies
could muster. Each of us took the part of an entire side, so in all
they had to dismiss me ten times before my 'team' had finished its
innings. With our four teams involved it went on for weeks.

Tom Davis, a team-mate at Clifton, was another close friend
with whom I would practise, a more than useful left-arm quickie.
His parents, like those of Brian Anderson, and indeed most boys
at Clifton, lacked nothing financially; Tom lived in a magnificent
house in the best part of the city, adorned by a flagpole with a
gold nugget on top. His parents would invite groups of us there
for weekends, which apart from more chances to play cricket in
their vast gardens gave rise to some light-hearted gang warfare.
Our tomfoolery was always at its height at the Davis's Guy
Fawkes party, when with irresponsibility quite becoming for our
age the two gangs would hurl enormous bangers at each other
around the grounds. One year, the inevitable happened. A loud
explosion injured the eye of a boy called Cooney, who later went
to Durban High School with me. I can remember the screams of
pain and trying uselessly to stop the bleeding by splashing on

handfuls of cold water from the tap at the bottom of the garden. We had to call his mother, and though the actual damage was less than the amount of blood suggested, that ended the firework parties.

When there was no one else around, I would practise for hours on my own, from what I've read something common in the childhood of cricketers, hurling a ball against a wall and batting against the rebound. My 'net' was our garage, my 'bat' was just twelve inches long. In retrospect this must have been extremely good conditioning for the eye and the reflexes. I used a golf ball which when I threw it at the wall used really to fly at me on the bounce.

It didn't pay to miss because behind me was the open end of the garage. When I did, the golf ball went many a mile and I had to traipse after it. Unsophisticated pressure training, really. I played my solo game for batting practice only, though I was to become a regular bowler during my teens and could get the ball to break off the wall from either side. In my private world of concentration I was the batsman only; I would never let myself get out because I had assumed the bowler's role.

From time to time I would be taken to Kingsmead to add to my education in the game by watching first-class cricket. I'm sure that, like so many of the youngsters you see today intensely engaged in matches with dustbins and satchels as wickets in the lunch and tea intervals at county or provincial games, I was more interested in the gaps in play. I can remember, though, being one of the kids who used to yell in anticipation as Roy McLean walked out to bat; what a favourite he was, the South African Denis Compton of his time, all charisma, flowing shots—even the haircream!

Naturally enough I identified with the South African heroes, but I remember being fascinated by the reputation of Peter May when he captained the MCC tour in 1957, and I was mortified by his disastrous form in the Tests; in 10 completed innings he scratched together only 153 runs. Some years later I also felt deflated when I made a special trip to watch Norman O'Neill bat for Richie Benaud's International Cavaliers, against Natal.

O'Neill had captured my imagination with the stories of his buccaneering batting for Australia. I watched in disbelief as he played and missed against John Cole, poking around for half an hour for 2 or 3 at Kingsmead before trailing back to the pavilion. Only later, when I faced him myself in club cricket and became a team-mate of his in the Natal side, did I discover that John Cole was a formidable opponent. I don't think I've ever seen a bowler who could swing the ball as much as John. That day he almost turned O'Neill inside out, with a similar effect on the emotions of one fourteen-year-old spectator, whose sighs of disappointment must have echoed around the ground.

After that I confined my adulation to South Africans; at least if they failed they would be back another day. But days of unhappiness were like rainstorms in the Durban summer, rare and easily forgotten. I was surrounded by contentment; in cricket and rugby I had found enough happiness and exercise to satisfy the most restless of young spirits.

From then on if I wanted a change from sport and my friends, I stuck to Grandpa. He never failed me, but he must take a certain responsibility for my Bunter-like figure at the time, filling me with scrumptious steak and kidney pies, a speciality at the local bakery.

He even taught me to drive at an age when most kids are still battling with their first bicycle. Grandpa was the proud owner of a Morris 1000, which in 1957 or 1958 was a very fashionable vehicle. Naturally from day to day I would be a passenger in this car, which held a tremendous fascination for me. Equally naturally, I pestered and pestered to be given the chance to drive it. From what you have already learned of Percy's devotion to his grandson, you will not be at all surprised to know that in the end he agreed.

The first time was pure Buster Keaton. That model had a gear stick which was longer than my arm—awkward to manage, particularly since reverse and first gears were adjacent in the gearbox. Having listened attentively to his instructions about clutch control and gear positioning, I duly attempted to edge this coveted motor car backwards out on to the road. Instead I slipped it into first and crashed forward through the garage door!

Grandpa was less demoralised than I, and he used to take me for long drives along the coast road, using the theory that he could trust my steering once he had got me through the gears up into top. I could not have been happier to be in command—perhaps an overstatement—of this machine that I had eyed so lovingly. My happiness totally overcame any apprehension.

Of course, it was all highly illegal, but Grandpa had his answer to that as well. He was one of these chaps who always used to wear a battered old trilby; you see them in most countries. His hat had become something of a trademark, and all the locals who never saw him indoors would never have known whether he had a hair on his head. The trilby had another use.

Whenever on our jaunts up the coast road we spied a police car, Grandpa would whip off his hat and thrust it on my head—sometimes pushing down so vigorously that I could barely see the road. But if I could not see the law, they certainly could not recognise that it was a twelve-year-old at the helm.

Occasionally I would take a chance and cheekily touch the peak in acknowledgement as they passed. After all, it had been Grandpa who had drummed in the lesson that it was only good manners to do so!

Chapter 3

When the Sun Always Shone

A quick succession of changes now disturbed the idyllic world of my early childhood. In due course I left prep school, exchanging the comfort of Clifton for the rigour of Durban High School. At around the same time the family moved house from the tranquillity of Davdon Court to another flat in Hampton Court on Durban's beachfront. My age, and the proximity of the sea with its infinite possibilities for exercise, induced another change: I shed the puppy-fat and shot up five inches in a year.

The change of environment gave me no problems: the sea and the surf drew me magnetically. The educational changes were a disaster. In retrospect, some of the difficulties were entirely my fault. Blowing down a Bunsen burner so that the science teacher can get no response when he comes to light it is a trick of impudent schoolboys of every generation in every school; at DHS it was my speciality.

Yet I began with a disadvantage. In the first year each boy had two choices: Latin or History, Biology or Geography. At Clifton neither Latin nor Biology had been on the curriculum, so my hand was forced. Maths became another problem because in the first year, before I had had a chance to settle down, we had no less than seven different masters—and for the last term none at all. This was a formative year. Robbie Gray, a contemporary who is now a good friend, has so much flair for the subject that he has become a well-respected chartered accountant. But even he failed the exams at the end of the first year. So you can guess what chance I had!

For maths my marks fluctuated between 0 and 19 per cent. For science, it was the same story. In the end in an effort to make up on the other subjects I took to cribbing—and of course I got caught! The night before one particular examination I had laboriously copied an essay answer in minute scrawl on to a piece of paper a couple of inches square. The idea was to conceal this answer in my palm.

The next day the right question duly appeared on the examination paper. Though I knew I was doing wrong, failure, even then, frightened me and this was one paper I was really going to kill. The trouble was I couldn't read my miniature handwriting! Gradually the distance between my hand and my eyes got closer and closer and I bent over my illegal aid.

I was just beginning to come to terms with the details when I looked up and caught the master's eye. Now I was a very, very bad liar; I had been brought up far too well for that. So of course my face went as red as a traffic light; it was a complete giveaway. The master hauled me out and I got o—out of 300 I think it was—another educational catastrophe.

So I spent the rest of my time at DHS in the 'B' classes. I think the main problem was that I found the teaching so boring; even today there are few subjects which can hold my attention for very long. This constant changing of teachers must have also contributed to my lack of interest. Very seldom in fact did we have the same master through a complete year of any of the set subjects.

I couldn't wait for the final bell of each day to come around; and the beach gave extra pleasure to my out-of-school hours. On hot days the journey home was wearisomely long. School ended at two forty-five, which became three by the time that I had prepared my books for homework. Then I had to walk to catch a bus into town and change buses for home. Usually it was past four o'clock when I clattered into the apartment, but it would only be a fleeting visit—just the two or three minutes it took to get into my bathing costume and pick up my surfboard.

I became an obsessive swimmer and board-rider. Most of the swimming took place in an enormous pool on the front; I worked up to three thousand yards a day and I suppose it was no surprise that I lost weight. With my father, I would begin at six o'clock in the morning—a thousand yards before school; then another thousand as soon as I got home, and the final stint later in the evening just before they closed the pool. It was a hundred yards long and I used to do ten lengths; it could be quite discouraging on your eighth or ninth length when you looked up to see if you were near the end, and you were only halfway with the rail a mere blur in the distance.

I became pals with two surfers who taught me about board-riding; I couldn't have picked two better friends. George Thompson developed into a magnificent exponent of the sport, representing South Africa and coming way up the lists in the world championships. Tony Scott switched his attentions to paddle ski-ing and has achieved great renown for his ski marathons from Cape Town to Durban.

We all joined the local Surf Club, at which we spent many a delightful hour, but only after surviving some terrible initiations from the regular members, who were all six or seven years older than us. A thorough 'sanding' was the beginning, where a group of gleeful watchers held you down while sand was stuffed in your hair, in your ears, down your costume—everywhere. But the longest discomfort came from glass fibre, which itches a hundred times more naggingly than the worst gnat-bite, and which was applied to that area on your back which you cannot reach with either arm over your shoulders or from behind your back. It would drive you mad, and the only way to remove it was to rub your back frantically up against a wall.

Another part of the surfer's ritual, of course, is the inevitable encounter with sharks. My moment of terror arrived when a group of us failed to take immediate notice of the tell-tale fin. We had become blasé because the predominant big fish along the coast were porpoises—with fins but friendly. But porpoises continually dive, so that their fins are never continuously exposed. Only belatedly did I realise that this particular fin was not disappearing!

I just fought off panic sufficiently to dive flat on to my board, and fortunately a rescuing wave pulled me into the shore. I remember not daring to stand up, even in the shallows, for fear my legs would be bitten from me. I waited until the board had glided all the way up the beach and the subsiding wave had left me high, dry and shaking before I jumped off and ran like hell to warn the lifeguard. A few seconds later and a story might have broken which could have led to *Jaws* being written by a South African, and Natal and Hampshire being short of a batsman.

But that alarming experience only heightened my ambitions. To my parents' bewilderment I became determined to leave school and become a lifesaver. All that sunshine, sand and surf had a Utopian air, and as I continually reassured my anxious mother, the shark was an extremely infrequent visitor. A career in cricket was so far-fetched as never to be considered.

Not that my enthusiasm had diminished. My father, realising that his lack of knowledge of the game could thwart my development, provided me with a coach in his friend Alan Butler. Alan played for Durban Technical College, a club side, along with Trevor Goddard. In retrospect his influence on my cricket, coming at such a formative time, probably enabled me to cross the line from club to first-class player.

Nor did he spoil me. Unlike my schooling, there was nothing boring about education in cricket. Two or three times a week I would happily cross the town to join in at the Tech nets; sometimes I'd go five times in a row waiting optimistically for a turn to bat, only to find that the light or a supply of bowlers failed me. But just fielding with the senior players I found captivating; sometimes I'd come home bruised from persuading one of the club players to throw catches to me when it was too dark to see the ball.

How much time I had with Alan depended on his other commitments but he would always help this pestering kid whenever he could; and if he had an hour and a half to spare I would receive his undivided attention. You can still see his influence in my batting today. He spent many evenings working on my grip on the bat, giving me natural feel with my left hand, the top and guiding hand on the grip for a right-hander. He used to insist that I held it right round the front, which was far from comfortable but did lead me to a textbook style of batting; a lot of players settle for a more practical grip with that hand further around the back of the bat.

He really attacked the basics of my batting. The Berea, that hill that overlooks the centre of Durban, used to be very visible from the nets, which led to a catch-phrase. If I didn't play a shot correctly with my right elbow up in the accepted position, Alan would yell 'Your shoulder's over the Berea again.' I must have heard it a thousand times until I began to get it right, but his patience with me remained inexhaustible.

Alan's philosophy of tuition made me into a back-foot player. He insisted on this and on the true pitches in South Africa it provided the means to make the transition from a tubby prep school batsman to a stringy run-scorer in High School cricket; only later did the special demands of English pitches, used so skilfully by seam bowlers in county cricket, alter my priorities.

Trevor Goddard, naturally, was deeply involved with his own career, but added a dash of colour to the picture of my development. At the time he represented something very special in South African cricket, arguably the best all-rounder we have ever produced. To the mature mind he was a celebrity; in my adolescence I held him in absolute awe. Yet he never patronised me, though I just couldn't grow used to him speaking to me as an equal. I used to stammer and blush when I replied, and it was always an over-respectful 'Mr Goddard' when I could find the words to address him. This type of reverence was to stay with me for a long time: when I later won my place in the full Natal side, I spoke to my captain as 'Mr McGlew' for two full seasons, before he took me into a quiet corner and announced that I had known him long enough to call him Jackie.

At school, as my studies stumbled from one disaster to the next, I could only make my mark through cricket. As a regular in the under-14, under-15 and then games for the 1st XI as a fifteen-year-old it brought me immense happiness and considerable friendship; it also brought tragedy into my life for the first time.

I first came across Anthony Cumberland as an opponent at Clifton, but we joined forces at DHS; as a steady little seamer he won a regular place in under-14 and under-15 XIs. More than that, we became firm friends, even though he lived several miles away in Durban North. But one day his parents came home to find him dead, hanging behind the door. Nobody ever found out what really happened; the most accepted theory was that he had climbed up on a chair to tie something up and had slipped; it couldn't have been deliberate.

It was one of the first funerals I had ever attended; the whole class went, but Tony had been my special buddy. I was simply crippled with a sadness that lasted for a very long time. In turn we filed past the open coffin where Tony lay as though he were simply fast asleep. I just wanted to put my hand on his shoulder to touch him and wake him up, to say 'Come on, it's time to go out and play.'

Chapter 4

Clay Casts a Shadow

My first indication that all was not right in South Africa came from an illustrious source. In July 1963 the then Cassius Clay was in London to defend his World Heavyweight title against Henry Cooper. I was on my first trip overseas as a member of the South African Schoolboys' tour. Our paths crossed in Tottenham Court Road.

A number of our party were on our way back to the YMCA, our city billet, when we spotted Clay and his manager Angelo Dundee outside the Sportsman's Club. The World Champion has, of course, never been bashful in public and he was happily entertaining a growing throng, signing autographs and doubtlessly informing the London public in which round Cooper was going to be beaten. Naturally, we joined the line to get close to a man we had heard so much about but never seen.

Gradually we edged nearer until Brian Surtees, our wicketkeeper, thrust his way to the very front, just ahead of me. Brian could hardly contain himself as he asked for the prized autograph, but Cassius detected an unfamiliar accent in the question and wanted to know where we were from. He was halfway through the signature when Brian replied 'South Africa'.

No punch could have stopped the champion in his tracks as abruptly as those two words. His head shot up from the piece of paper; his eyes widened as he glared suspiciously at us. Then, just as quickly, he finished the autograph, pushed the paper back at Surtees and turned away to the other side of the crowd. No more than three feet away from his face, I had a perfect view of his distaste at the mention of my country.

We all felt embarrassed, and though we stayed just to be close to a man we admired, no one spoke to him. The incident was soon pushed into the back of our naïve minds and I can remember all the party watching the fight on television as he beat Cooper. No one considered that his reaction was a foretaste of the growing opinion which in the end would mar the cricket careers of a number of the tourists.

The trip to England came as a culmination of my efforts at Durban High School, where I had begun to mature as a batsman. I had a stroke of luck too, which took me into the good books of Les Theobald, the master in charge of cricket at DHS. Harry Crabtree, the old Essex player and coach, had come to Durban on a world tour setting examinations for school teachers to become registered coaches. Theo took me to the nets as one of his guinea-pigs while he attempted to pass Mr Crabtree's examination. I played well. Theo got his certificate. From then on I think he had a soft spot for me.

Theo set his standards very high; in that respect he led me along the right lines. The war had interfered with his own playing career, but he too had been a promising young player and had come close to South African honours at schoolboy level. He might not have been amongst the best cricketers in the world, but he would be way up on the list of the best-dressed; immaculate creases in his flannels, his shirt beautifully ironed, his boots shining white.

He took me as a fifteen-year-old into the DHS 1st XI in January 1961, and within one marvellously exciting year I was to play for South African Schools. On the way, I was on the right end of a typical illustration of Theo's attitude towards the manners of the game. In one of the first matches for DHS where I had already been moved up from a tenderfoot No. 10 to bat at No. 3 I faced my Clifton buddy Tom Davis, who had moved to Sir Henry's School.

Tom was still very much the star bowler, and against us soon got among the wickets again. Early in my innings he dipped an inswinger into me, right on the back foot. I almost walked, because I was so plumb lbw. Tom had never lacked ferocity, and he leapt six feet in the air roaring a raucous appeal that would make Dennis Lillee's notorious shouts sound like a polite inquiry. To everyone's disbelief, especially my own, Theo said not out.

I went on to make our top score with 35; and though Tom finished with 6 for 34 and Sir Henry's beat us by 4 wickets, murmuring inquests on my lbw appeal were still continuing after the game. Eventually Tom approached Theo and suggested that it must have been very close. 'When you learn to appeal with a little decorum, young man, you might get a decision,' Theo replied.

Schools cricket in Durban is structured each year around two major events, the Offord Week and the Nuffield Week. The Offord week takes place in the Christmas holidays, a jamboree of one-day matches between all the most accomplished cricketing schools in Natal. From the performances during this festival a squad of Natal players is chosen to represent the province in the Nuffield Week; success there can lead to the highest accolade of all, selection for the South African Schools XI, which plays a full province side. Somehow in my first attempt at this considerable prize I stayed the course.

The previous year I had watched DHS play in the Offord Week with all the wide-eyed ambition of a schoolboy. Actually to make the side in December 1961 represented the fulfilment of an ambition in itself. At nearly sixteen and a half I still had time to wait for a place in the Natal Schools squad. But when they announced the party of thirteen my name appeared on the list. Nor was I the youngest; Mike Smithyman, whose parents lived in Zanzibar and who attended Michaelhouse, was two months my junior, and the squad was made up by a round-faced fifteen-year-old, still described as a 'batsman/wicket-keeper', named M. J. Procter.

At that time his arrival just made one more familiar face; Prockie spent most of his time with his elder brother Anton, a medium-pace bowler. On my first long cricket trip I kept closer company with the two other boys from DHS, the fast-developing Lee Irvine and Harvey Wannenberg. Though for one or two of our squad the overnight trip to Johannesburg for the 1962 Nuffield Week provided the ideal opportunity for an illicit smoke in the corridor or a beer when the manager's back was turned, I was taking no risks. If I couldn't sleep, it was only because I was too excited at the prospect of the forthcoming matches.

I soon discovered that I had no monopoly of youthful promise. In Natal's opening game, staged on the Wanderers' No. 3 ground, a fourteen-year-old added extra precociousness where there was already plenty about. Hylton Ackerman's boyish looks may have fooled our bowlers; they certainly knew all about him at the end of the match when Ackie was 101 not out, with Border beating us by 6 wickets.

Hylton's innings was the first large-scale announcement of the rich talents which were to take him into Currie Cup and county cricket. Selected for the cancelled tour of Australia in 1971–72, he would be high on the list of those whose international careers were sacrificed to politics. That year he experienced a remarkable week of ups and downs which must partly have prepared him for the disappointments of later life. He had that brilliant hundred against us plus two other reasonable scores, but his three other innings of the week, one of them the last against the full Transvaal side, all took place at that Mecca of South African cricket, the Wanderers' main stadium. In all three Ackie failed to score.

My best performance came on the Thursday, a steady 65 in a rearguard action against Transvaal Schools in the main stadium where Ackie had been so jinxed. Bolstered by a couple of other medium-sized scores, I realised that I was on the fringe of, but by no means a certainty for, the South African Schools side. All the competing players gathered at the close of play on the Friday to hear the selectors' choice. With a deep breath and a nibble of my nails I stood at the back as the following team was read out: R. M. Nicholson (Natal) (Captain), H. M. Ackerman (Border), J. L. Breedt (Transvaal), F. Kalk (Transvaal), T. McDonald (Border), R. S. M. Melville (Natal), C. J. B. Nourse (Rhodesia), B. A. Richards (Natal), K. J. Tonkin (Rhodesia), N. R. Weightman (Transvaal), B. H. Williams (Rhodesia).

Of course we could not hold a candle to the full Currie Cup Transvaal side the following day. Arthur Tayfield, brother of Hugh, struck 98 and we were all ill-equipped to cope with their bowling. I managed 9 before I dragged on to my stumps a ball from Slug Lodwick, who was considerably quicker than any bowler I had faced up to that time. Nevertheless, I was left with the gratifying memory of having appeared on the same field as the legendary John Waite and the rising star Ali Bacher.

Of our side only Hylton and myself graduated into professional ranks, although Chris Nourse, the wicket-keeper, tried his luck in

England and had a couple of summers on the Hampshire staff. Freddie Kalk made his name on the soccer field, while I still see Robin Melville on my travels: he has literally made a career in higher circles, as a jumbo jet pilot.

I never talked to Lee Irvine about his omission from that side, but he returned to school cricket with the fervour of a man with a point to prove. His bat was the main weapon as DHS slaughtered all the neighbouring schools; it brought him 123, 125 not out, and 122 in three successive innings, two scores of 96, and relative failures of 67 and 41; he averaged 96·86. If you wanted brighter cricket, you had to shield your eyes from the glare of our run-making: 304 for 4 declared in 136 minutes against Kearsney; 239 for 3 declared in 145 minutes against Glenwood; 253 for 2 declared in 138 minutes against Hilton, when Lee and I added 197 for the 2nd wicket. We were bettered only once, by Wilfred Isaacs' XI which was sprinkled with Test players.

These were memories enough to keep us warm during the winter, which for me weighed like lead in my shoes. I couldn't wait to sample again the joys I had tasted the previous year. The very smell of more cricket lessened the disappointment of an enforced change of base. Hampton Court, my beachfront haven, had been condemned for demolition; early next summer we would have to move inland again.

In the end Mum and Dad settled on a rent-controlled flat in Gordon Road; by coincidence the block was called Nuffield Court. We took up new residence at the same time that plans were being finalised for the Nuffield Week of 1963, to be the forerunner of a Nuffield Tour to England the following summer. Now every young player in the country had a firm target in mind.

With such incentives DHS was just as successful over the 1962–63 season with Lee's crushing strokeplay in the vanguard, and Bruce Heath, younger brother of Natal's Grayson, providing the support. Howard Carpendale won an occasional spot lower down the order, but he was destined for success in a quite different field. His keenness edged him into the 1st XI, but his real talent was for singing. He became the vocalist in the school pop group, The Strangers, all of whom later travelled to England to try to break into the big time.

Unfortunately, in their rush to make their first million, they forgot little essentials like work permits and the British customs wouldn't let them in. All but Howard found their way back home, but he travelled on to Germany where he has become one of their most popular singers. His sister married an Englishman and lives in Southampton; in 1976 he had scheduled a cruise on the *QE2* as a holiday, and on a brief visit to his sister he found out that Hampshire were playing Sussex at Hove. To the utter mystification of his German-born wife he insisted on watching until I was out. Unfortunately he caught me on one of my better days; I made 136 and he had to jump on board the *QE2* as they were pulling up the gangplank.

Howard, the cricketer, did not make the squad for the Offord Week back in December 1962, which began for DHS with a win over Maritzburg College in which I baffled a number of tail-enders—and certainly myself—in a spell of 4 for 1, with my gentle off-spinners. Lee again played a forceful role and at the end of the week he was chosen to lead the Natal Schools into the Nuffield Week, that year to be held in Cape Town.

Bruce Heath, Brian Anderson and Harvey Wannenberg brought the DHS contingent up to five, and for Harvey and myself selection was only the prelude to another thrill. On the afternoon of New Year's Eve 1962 the majority of South Africans were pre-occupied with preparations for the festivities of the evening, but Harvey and I were shifting nervously from one foot to another at the Kingsmead nets as we listened attentively to the counsel of a cricketing legend.

Denis Compton was sheltering in Durban from the English winter. Just how be came to be addressing two extremely lucky schoolboy cricketers that day has always remained a mystery to me. Wilfred Isaacs, that splendid benefactor to the South African game, was involved somewhere along the line; Compo's arm, which propelled several of his famed chinamen and googlies at me, showed no sign of having been twisted by Theo, whom Denis knew through Wilfred; but I'm sure it was. Mrs Wannenberg watched proudly from a distance, and I suspect that her social connections had been brought into play as well.

Whatever the reason, I batted, Harvey bowled and Denis gave us both some gentle coaching. His presence had the same stupe-fying effect on me as that of Trevor Goddard and Jackie McGlew.

48

I cannot remember a word of what he said to us—the same encouraging message he would give to any youngsters, I suspect. But he became a great champion of mine, and on later visits to Durban he was to be quoted as advocating my inclusion in the South African Test side.

That memorable afternoon provided a perfect stimulus for a Nuffield Week that became a personal triumph. I began with 82 against Griqualand West in a match we won by 205 runs, took 50 off Rhodesia, and then everything fell into place with 102 against Western Province and 101 off North-East Transvaal. The first hundred came in tandem with Mike Procter, as we sailed into the Western Province attack with a partnership of 164 in 81 minutes; Prockie had reached 102 not out at the declaration. Some of Compo's batting magic must have rubbed off on Harvey, because he helped himself to 56 not out against North-Eastern Transvaal in an unbroken 8th-wicket stand with Tom Davis, who was in his first Nuffield Week.

This time I don't think it is immodest to say that I expected to have my name read out for the South African Schools XI on the Friday evening. Lee's world was put to rights when he was announced as captain and Prockie too came into the side for the first time; Hylton, by now all of fifteen and a half, retained his place; and Mike Burton of Rhodesia, Tony Biggs of Eastern Province and Robbie Muzzell of Border, all of whom were to play first-class cricket, helped make up one of the strongest Schoolboy XIs for many a year.

Even so, Transvaal had clearly shown themselves to be on a higher level in the representative match a year earlier, and Western Province represented a mountainous task. In Kelly Seymour and Harry Bromfield they had two off-spinners who were to play for their country; Peter van der Merwe was to lead South Africa in winning series against England and Bobby Simpson's Australians; Gerald Innes had toured Australia in 1952–53; John Rushmere was a respected opening bowler and his partner Hamish Miller later played for Glamorgan in the County Championship.

Their own confidence was reflected in a declaration which left us to make 237 to win in 226 minutes. When time ran out we lost our final wicket for 341, having batted on following an official

3-wicket victory gained with more than three-quarters of an hour to spare. Lee set the course with a rapid 40, John Festing of Border steered us home with 52 not out, and I reached my third century in successive days, 106 before I was caught by John White off Kelly Seymour. In the most decisive manner, though admittedly helped by a generous declaration, we had become rare schoolboy winners against a provincial side. I don't believe the feat has been repeated since. The cuttings in my scrapbook tell me that I was only the fourth schoolboy to take a hundred off a provincial attack, though Peter Kirsten has followed in my footsteps.

Of course I was showered with telegrams; newspapers splashed headlines of such lavish praise that even now make me blush to read them; some journalists seemed to think I had supernatural powers. Fortunately at school I had seen too many big-heads cruelly, if quite properly, deflated. I kept my proudest thoughts to myself; my fear of overshooting the required low profile even controlled my clothing. When I returned from Cape Town I was awarded my honours blazer for cricket, a rank even higher than 1st XI colours; that blazer, with its extra gold braid, remained in my wardrobe for several weeks in case I should be thought conceited for wearing it.

Had I needed a swift return to earth, a salutary experience awaited me when I was selected for my début in club cricket. Eventually, those long, happy evenings with Alan Butler at the Tech nets were to pull me to that club, but while still at school I appeared for Durban High School Old Boys.

It could hardly have been more inauspicious. I prodded about on a wet wicket like an absolute novice, and I think I was dropped twice before someone hung on at slip to put me out of my misery for 3. But I also forgave Norman O'Neill, because the Hoy Park bowler who continually found the edges of my bat was the same John Cole who had so demoralised my Australian hero. I now found out what an extremely talented bowler Cole was.

Though we had Test players like Colin Wesley and Dennis Gamsy in our side, John ruthlessly cut us to pieces. Colin had toured England with the 1960 Springboks, and an apocryphal story was spread about the beginning of his Test career. Apparently Don Bradman had been in England for that series, and Colin had met him after scoring 0 in his first Test innings. Then

Don placed a reassuring arm around his shoulder and said,
'Don't worry, we've all done that.' Colin duly got o in the
second innings, and asked Bradman 'Did you ever do that?' 'No,
I was never that good,' was the quick reply.

The truth is that Colin Wesley scored 11 and 35 in his first
Test, at Lord's, the 35 being top score in a total of 137 in a South
African débâcle which will only be remembered for the no-balling
of Geoff Griffin for throwing. His pair came in the next Test at
Trent Bridge when Brian Statham dismissed him first ball in
both innings, the bowler's third triumph against Colin in his
four visits to the crease. Of course this considerably amused his
team-mates, and when Colin was chosen for the Fourth Test
they sent him a telegram saying: 'Congratulations on your selection. Looking forward to seeing you. Brian Statham.'

The prospect of the tour to England now shone like a guiding
star, and grew more enticing in February, when the programme of
twenty-two matches in thirty-five days was finally announced; I
was named as one of twenty-seven optimistic young cricketers for
trials in Johannesburg at the end of the month—two days of nets
plus a one-day game against Richie Benaud's Cavaliers.

Bill Alley and Brian Surtees, who kept wicket for them because
of an injury to Roy Swetman, were the only non-Test players in
Benaud's side, though a declaration which set us 286 to win in
140 minutes could hardly be called a 'Cavalier' one; only when I
had played the game a little longer did I understand the reasoning
that as a professional the less fielding you have to do the better!

We succumbed in fact to the unorthodox spin bowling of David
Sincock, a mesmeric mixture of chinamen and googlies; he spun
the ball like a top but had insufficient control to become a bowler
of true international class. Prockie profited by the inevitable loose
deliveries, racing to a splendid 76 in an hour which settled his
seat on the plane to England. I batted with him in a partnership
of 57 in 31 minutes as we set out in vain after Richie's declaration.

So when the selectors announced the fifteen names that evening
I fully expected to be on the list. I was not, however, prepared to
find my name at the top of the touring party: B. A. Richards
(Natal) (Captain), M. J. Procter (Natal), (Vice-Captain), H. M.
Ackerman (Border), A. L. Biggs (E. Province), T. D. Cullinan

(E. Province), K. I. Deutschmann (Border), M. B. Heath (Natal), D. R. Lindsay-Smith (Transvaal), R. E. T. Morris (W. Province), G. N. Ridley (Rhodesia), N. Rosendorff (Orange Free State), M. J. Smithyman (Natal), B. V. T. Surtees (Orange Free State), A. G. van Wyk (E. Province), G. L. G. Watson (Transvaal).

I had Brian Surtees to thank for my totally unexpected elevation to the leadership. His immaculate wicket-keeping as a stand-in for the Cavaliers had edged him in front of Justin White, who had captained and kept wicket for the Schools XI. In fact I would take the role of deputy wicket-keeper myself. Like everyone but the selectors I had assumed that Justin would lead the touring party; yet his crushing disappointment was nowhere near the surface when he was one of the first to congratulate the selected players and myself. Though this unanticipated challenge added a stimulating dimension to the tour, the news that Les Theobald and Jackie McGlew would co-manage the trip allayed my considerable apprehension.

In fact I only had to wait two days before I first led my new side into the field, because this frantic week ended with a trip to Pietermaritzburg where the Nuffield XI were pitched in against a full-strength Natal XI. Considering the emotional and geographical upheavals of the previous week, it was hardly surprising that we lost by 6 wickets. Unabashed the party dispersed homewards, and each member ticked off the days on the nearest calendar until June 8th, when we were to reassemble in Johannesburg.

For fifteen young South Africans from a variety of backgrounds, the five weeks in England were to provide a crash course in experience, much of it connected with cricket, but in terms of our collective knowledge of life we were rookies being sent to the front line. The captain began in fine fashion in that respect; the camera lovingly provided by my parents to record the trip snapped gleefully away as we stopped at Brazzaville airport— but I'd forgotten to take it out of its case. As I say, there was much to learn.

As a group we were as mixed as a bag of fruit drops. Prockie and Ackie had grown close buddies by now; together they were not above tying up their sheets in the dormitories we stayed in and disappearing down the makeshift rope into the night. Dassie Biggs, on the other hand, would always toe the line. Dave

Cullinan was another with a mischievous streak, a perky little character whose family had connections with the famous Cullinan diamond.

Kevin Deutschmann was what we called a 'Cho', standing for Cricket Hours Only; we rarely saw him the rest of the time, a real mystery man. Mike Smithyman, too, I never really could fathom: I would set a field for his bowling with six fielders on the off and he would fire the ball outside the leg stump; then, if you took him to task, he just would not understand—a captain's nightmare but a fine cricketer.

Giles Ridley, who later went to Oxford University, was a very studious type even then; he used to astound us by spending the little time we had away from cricket at museums and art galleries; we soon discovered that he was the perfect man for receptions, where he would deflect the boring officials away from the rest of us.

Bruce Heath became the butt of most of our humour, the usual schoolboy pranks of sausage rolls jammed into his cricket boots, and apple-pie beds. There was no nicer guy on the trip than Dick Morris, with a sense of humour as dry as dust. Neil Rosendorff was the quiet man while few made more noise than Brian Surtees, a joker whose impressions of the South African broadcaster Charles Fortune could make a statue smile.

Duncan Lindsay-Smith as the youngest, had the widest eyes of all; he just could not believe that Soho was real, and often led the volunteers to walk back from nets at Lord's to our base in Tottenham Court Road, so he could take another peep. Our general naïveté was best summed up when van Wyk, one of our seniors, solemnly returned a handkerchief at a dance to a young lady who had to explain to him why she had dropped it. 'Chaka' Watson had the least inhibitions; as rough as a bear, he had never been outside Johannesburg, and he meant to leave his mark on England.

I had left no cover over the lens of my mind's eye; images remain sharply in focus. The first television any of us had ever seen was actually in the bus which collected us from Heathrow airport; the thrill of our first nets at Lord's; the genuine surprise when we found our rooms at the YMCA in Tottenham Court Road, innocently left unlocked, had been rifled by thieves.

At Lord's, in the nets at the Nursery End, Hylton Ackerman celebrated his first visit to cricket's headquarters with a massive blow which broke a window in a house some hundred yards away. Anxious as ever for diplomacy, Jackie McGlew sent Bruce Heath on a dual mission to pacify the owner and collect the ball. In fact the lady was far from amused, even though, as instructed, Bruce insisted that compensation would be forthcoming. Finally being on the wrong end of her wrath struck a raw nerve. 'It wasn't me who hit it,' said our opening batsman. 'It was that chap batting in the nets now.' The lady peered across Lord's; then she smiled: 'But he's a left-hander, so he must have hit the ball over long-off. What a fine stroke! Oh, forget about the window!'

As captain my leadership was confined to the field of play. The norm in South African education is that boys do not look up to other boys, only to masters. Jackie and Theo selected the side for each match, so my responsibilities were restricted to the pitch. The regular cricket answer in reply to the question 'What makes a good captain?' is 'A good side'. As a seventeen-year-old novice skipper I was fortunate enough to have an extremely good side.

Of our twenty-one games we won ten, drew nine and were beaten only twice—in our first match against Oxford Authentics when, in our keenness, we stayed on the field in a torrential downpour; and against the Lord's Taverners where we contributed to our own downfall. Van Wyk, who had been 'borrowed' by our hosts, hung on to a brilliant catch on the boundary to dismiss Gary Watson at a crucial phase of the match.

After visits to bat manufacturers, where free kit was kindly supplied, we embarked on a whistle-stop tour around the public school and bank sides, mainly in the south of England. Nobody worried that the intensity of the cricket meant that there was little time for orthodox sightseeing; we were so keen that regularly after we had finished the scheduled match we would amuse ourselves with a pick-up game on the outfield with a chair as a wicket. Jackie McGlew must have been impressed with our enthusiasm until we persuaded him to join in one evening. Prockie's party trick was to bowl left-handed, and one of his cunning deliveries broke the co-manager's finger!

Much of the fun looking back on the tour is in noting some of the eminent English players in the making whom we encountered.

Richard Gilliat, later to become my county captain, was in the Charterhouse side that Morris and Ridley bowled out in no time at all. There we were amazed to find beer on the table for the players at lunchtime, which to our way of life seemed extremely lax; one or two of their side batted as though they had abused the privilege, while we stuck to orange squash. Graham Roope at Bradfield and Roger Tolchard at Malvern were others we played against at the start of careers which led on to Test cricket; we had heard plenty about Tolchard, who was being tipped to be an England player, though in fact he had to wait over thirteen years before he finally played in a Test Match on England's tour to India in 1976-77.

At Bradfield rain finished the match early in the day, which provided the excuse for a feast of strawberries and cream—a really English occasion in a marquee in the college grounds. We had never seen such large strawberries; I had at least six enormous helpings. Nor had we ever seen squirrels, which raced around the outskirts of the pitch. The challenge proved too much for 'Chaka' Watson, who became determined to catch one with his bare hands so that we could have a closer look. I have never been back to Bradfield since, but the picture will never leave my mind of sitting in the marquee in front of a mountain of strawberries watching Chaka vainly charging from one side to another in pursuit of a squirrel; he even took off like a rocket to follow one up a tree.

On the field few of our adversaries got away; only rain stopped us from winning our first real test, against the MCC Young Professionals, where Chaka turned his abundant energies to a more productive purpose by hitting a promising West Indian new ball bowler, Wes Stewart, for three towering sixes, all out of the Chiswick ground and two so far that we never found the balls.

But it was the prospect of facing a more notorious fast bowler from the West Indies which almost unnerved us. We travelled down to Millfield School in Somerset to play an XI selected by the headmaster, R. J. O. Meyer, to find that we were facing Roy Gilchrist. Gilchrist's reputation was at that time for bouncers and even beamers delivered with total hostility; once hailed as the fastest bowler in the world, he was known to burn a short fuse.

Gilchrist had driven down for the day, from his League commitments in Lancashire, because he specially wanted some batting practice. Even the most confident of our number thought they spotted the first smoulderings when Mr Meyer declared just as his opening bowler was walking to the wicket. It seemed an act calculated to produce fire from the dragon's nostrils.

Dassie Biggs and Brian Surtees opened for us, with survival rather than a win on their minds. After fending off a couple of bumpers Brian was caught at short leg off his glove; he just mumbled incoherently as he passed me. The ground was scarcely big enough to accommodate Gilchrist's run-up; he used to bowl like an uncoiling spring because he stood only about 5 ft 7 in, but would leap into the delivery stride. I took a somewhat trembling guard, and during the time he took to run in two pieces of advice from Trevor Goddard flashed through my mind: 'Go back to give yourself time to see the ball' and 'Shorten the backlift to get the bat down in time.' Whether I acted out those tips I'll never know, but the ball shot off my bat towards point and I set off like a March hare for the quickest single I have ever taken in my life.

He trapped me lbw in the end, but we all coped reasonably well and, taking advantage of some charitable spinners in the middle of the innings, beat them, Gilchrist and all, by 4 wickets. If the West Indian had left me one or two bruises to my body, my pride was soon to be more greatly damaged—by an Australian.

Peter May captained the Lord's Taverners against us at the Oval, but Richie Benaud made the most impression. I moved my score on from 33 to 37 by clobbering through mid-wicket a leg-break that he dropped short; I had faced him before in the Cavaliers game prior to the tour and just for a second my confidence outstripped my ability. Richie needed not a moment more; he pitched another short ball in the same spot. I hardly had time to enjoy the feeling of the prospect of another boundary when the ball ripped into my stumps before I had even begun the down-swing of my shot. Of course he hadn't bowled the leg-break but the 'flipper' or top-spinner which just hit the deck and fizzed straight through. The newspaper report recorded: 'Richards made an unworthy swipe at Benaud and was bowled.' In fact the cunning fox had seen a precocious schoolboy cross his path and quietly took him to the cleaners; just a reminder that I still had plenty to learn.

Lord's offered kinder memories. The mild opposition of the

touring Canadian Colts could not detract from the awesome feeling of walking out to bat there for the first time. My 59 against bowling as tepid as Roy Gilchrist's had been torrid will always be assured of a corner in my store of recollections, coming as it did just a week after we had reverently watched England play the West Indies in the legendary Test where Ted Dexter struck a glorious 70, Brian Close deliberately took bouncers from Wes Hall and Charlie Griffith on his torso and Colin Cowdrey had to come in with a broken arm to save England from defeat.

The climax to the tour came with four games against county 2nd XIs or representative sides. Warwickshire 2nd XI fielded a B. A. Richardson, which amused me at the time; only later did I find out that he was the youngest brother of Peter and Dick, who both played for England, Peter who took 498 minutes to reach a hundred in Johannesburg in 1956, at the time the slowest century in Test cricket. Rain at Edgbaston rescued the professional side.

Though I was not to know it at the time, the next match was to play more than a passing role in my future. Hampshire 2nd XI at Southampton was just another fixture on the card. As was the lordly custom of our professional opponents, we were put in to bat first, and Bob Cottam, who was later to become my room-mate on the county circuit, opened with a maiden to Dave Cullinan. Neil Rosendorff then fell to the second ball of the second over from Peter Haslop and I hit the remaining four balls for four.

I finished with 79, probably my most fluent innings of the tour. I suppose it came up for re-analysis five years later when the welcome mat was stretched out for overseas players. At the time I can only recall being furious because we felt we had an lbw wrongly turned down off the last ball of the match when they were 9 wickets down.

At Old Trafford I committed the folly of the innocent by sending both my sweaters away for cleaning at the same time; on yet another afternoon when rain interrupted our victory charge, the hardened members of the Lancashire XI must have thought I was mad as I strolled to the wicket in just shirt and flannels. A last-wicket stand by Nottinghamshire 2nd XI thwarted what would have been another notable victory at Trent Bridge, particularly after Prockie had played the innings of the tour, 130 not out, to rescue us after we slumped to 8 for 3 against Barry Stead and Andy Corran.

In the bars and tea tents up and down England we found very little comment hostile to South Africa. Many local people barely knew the geography of the continent; we could have been from North, West or East Africa for all they knew; in 1963 South Africa was not a daily fixture in the headlines of the world's press as it is today.

Our visit did precipitate a number of articles on the sports pages, some of which even went so far as to suggest the sort of ban on South African involvement in cricket that later came to pass. But it was heard as noises off rather than any sustained trumpeting of a cause.

Inevitably there must have been times when our schoolboy opponents questioned us on the policy of our government, though in my experience sports-loving youngsters find political discussions as appealing as being told to come indoors and do their homework. When you consider that several of our side were Afrikaners, considerably more right-wing than those of us from English backgrounds, there could have been an occasional vehement debate, but I was never present at one.

I defended South Africa down to the ground, with all the fervour one would expect from someone who had enjoyed the benefits of a system and who had never known any other lifestyle. If I was cross-questioned on the absence of a 'one man, one vote' system, I would glibly reply that it was impossible because black people were educationally inferior; after all some could not read or write. At that time I would never question *why* they were illiterate, or whose fault it was.

It would take me other visits before I could appreciate the injustices—and before I could fully understand why in front of a bunch of cricket-mad schoolboys who were having the time of their lives, Cassius Clay had turned his back.

Chapter 5

From Benoni to Bristol

If the flames had begun to die on my once burning ambition to earn a living sunning myself on a beachfront with a little life-saving thrown in to keep me from sunburn, I still looked upon professional cricket as a career for a fashionable few in the English county game. Despite a flickering interest from Essex and a more substantial approach from the MCC during the 1963 Nuffield tour, my sights remained firmly on playing first-class cricket for Natal.

In December that year I took my final leave of the teaching staff at DHS who were all of the opinion that as a scholar I was not a bad cricketer! I qualified for a final appearance in the Offord and Nuffield Weeks shortly after my last term. In view of my academic record, it was the only qualification I had!

The Nuffield Week provided a disarming experience, when I captained Natal Schools with Prockie again vice-captain. I began well with 55 in a match-winning partnership with Mike (72 not out) against Transvaal. But from then on it was as downhill as an Olympic ski event—3 against Western Province, 1 against Orange Free State followed by 0 against Eastern Province. My first really bad trot.

On reflection I am sure that I reacted to the pre-tournament publicity that I would command a place in the South African Schools side even if I failed. I certainly put that theory to the test. Yet the selectors did judge me on my past record, and named me captain for the final game of the week against North-Eastern Transvaal's provincial side. Eight of the side had toured England;

Hylton Ackerman and I became the first South African school-boys to win four caps.

The honour did nothing to repair my form. Jackie Botten, who then held the Currie Cup record for the most wickets in one season, 55 in 1958–59, and Sid Burke, who achieved the remarkable paradox of taking 11 wickets in his début Test against New Zealand in 1961 and then being dropped, were a formidable opening pair. Burke trapped me lbw for 1. Four days later, however, I pulled out of the slump with 50 for the SA Schools XI against the senior Western Province Invitation XI. If that set my immediate world to rights, I did not forget the lesson of the over-relaxation in the previous week.

The rest of the 1963–64 season I spent in grade cricket, now representing the Tech Club in the inter-city matches in Durban. In between games I began my confrontation with the usual problems facing the school-leaver and the teenager. I solved one with my first job, at the suggestion of Alan Butler, who may well have been trying to lessen the demands I placed upon him at the Tech nets. Alan suggested his own line, insurance.

I began as a clerk—in fact nothing more than a glorified tea boy—for the South African Mutual Insurance Company; for my toil in the fire and accident department I received 70 rand a month —before tax. Thirty rand of the remainder swiftly left my pocket for my mother's purse for my board, so I hardly offered a threat to the Rothschilds.

I also fell in love, with all the fervour and helplessness of one's first genuine affair. Her name was Penny, and I'd spotted her at the beachfront pool, where she was a regular visitor. I would go round to her house more evenings than not, and I'd often stay until I'd missed the last bus, which meant a lengthy walk home through some of the roughest parts of the city.

Our relationship lasted for some six or seven years, but I always felt in the back of my mind that getting married was for older people—though I bought a ring for a planned engagement on my twenty-first birthday. I suppose in the end I just got cold feet, an expensive change of heart because I had saved up over 100 rand for the ring; funnily enough my mother discovered it in a drawer not long ago, and now she wears the keepsake that Penny never received.

The combination of income and a steady girlfriend inevitably led to a quest for transport, at last fulfilling those fantasy days with Grandpa by owning a car of my own. For the princely sum of 50 rand, I finally settled for a 1950 Vauxhall, which was a real snip because over fourteen years it had done only 39,000 miles. I painted it and, much to my father's disgust, added the teenager's trimmings of stripes and flashes. The fact that it kept slipping out of second gear—which meant stopping, lifting up the bonnet and lining up a couple of joints—only added to my love of this big round saloon.

This was the first incident in a sequence of events in which to my own grief I discovered I was neither financially nor technologically equipped to attack the world of motor racing. Within a year the rather leisurely performance of the Vauxhall had become too much of a frustration; any sentimental feeling about the departure of a first car was soon obliterated by the satisfaction of a sale which brought me a 20 rand profit. I still needed parental help to come up with the replacement, a Mini Cooper which earned me a spot in the illicit drag-racing on the beachfront on Sunday nights in summer.

Just down the coast in Durban is a public road which runs straight for a mile and a half; when the highway was clear two cars would pull out side by side and the race would be on. No money changed hands; the prize was the tag of being 'the fastest car on the beach'. I had just one dabble, but in straining for an extra mile per hour the engine popped an oil seal, and because I had spent so much buying the Mini it was a long while before I could afford the labour to have this 70 cent seal replaced. I never did achieve my ambition, which was to race a saloon car on the Roy Hesketh circuit in Maritzburg.

But I retained an obsession with cars until another dream vehicle ripped holes in my bank balance—and almost into Penny and myself. My father's warnings as usual fell on deaf ears as I emptied all 1,200 rand of my savings into a converted Cortina embellished with racing accessories. Now I was sure I would become a boy wonder of the track. Sadly my funds would not stretch to replacing four rather worn tyres, nor could I pay a full insurance cover; I just had enough cents to provide the statutory third-party rate.

I was very keen to show off my new toy at a party out of town, particularly as I knew Prockie would be there with his own pride and joy, a new Viva. At this time Prockie shared a flat with Hylton Ackerman—an absolute disaster of an establishment; if ever you went to the fridge to look for something to eat you would find nothing but a jug of ice-cold water, the morning antidote for the after-effects of their favourite drink of cane and Coke.

The party turned out to be hopeless—too many uninvited guests and neither room nor drink to accommodate them. Penny and I decided to look elsewhere for our evening's entertainment, but got no further than the bottom of a ditch a mile up the road. The combination of an S-bend, an inverted camber, a surface greased by rain and my wearing tyres overcame my skill at the wheel. The Cortina lurched sideways down a ten-foot drop.

Fortunately Penny suffered no more than a bruised back which restricted her to sleeping in a sitting position for a night or two. I was totally unscathed physically, hit hard only by the realisation that my 1,200 rand had disappeared into the ditch with us. That shock kept me so still that Penny screamed out because she thought I was dead. The entire chassis of the car had gone off-centre, so that I had to belt the door with my elbow to free ourselves. The battery had been installed in the boot, another racing modification, and the impact of the crash had thrown it fifty yards away.

I couldn't believe my good fortune when the very first car which came round the bend as we scrambled back to the roadside was Prockie's new Viva. I found it harder to believe when I leapt out to flag him down and he drove unseeing past us, almost running me over. My car, of course, was a write-off, though I cut my losses with a visit to a friend who was an expert panel-beater; he welded the undamaged front end of my car on to the good back end of another smashed Cortina. I sold the hybrid vehicle, so if you're driving a Cortina, registration number ND 8080, I'd advise you to have a garage thoroughly check it out!

Less dramatic was my introduction to first-class cricket, in a friendly against Transvaal at Kingsmead at the start of the 1964–65 season. As a raw nineteen-year-old I was way down the batting order, and Roy McLean and Derek Varnals demolished the Transvaal attack. I did reach the stage of putting my pads on, but when Jackie McGlew declared I was still in the pavilion waiting my turn. We bowled them out twice in no time at all and won by an innings. Apart from my stint in the field I spent my time sitting shyly in the corner of the dressing-room, speaking only when spoken to.

I had only to wait a few days, until 30th October 1964, before I took guard for the first time in first-class cricket. Along with Dennis Gamsy and Richard Dumbrill from Natal I was chosen for the South African Colts XI to play against the MCC tourists at Benoni.

Ted Dexter led the visitors in place of the captain, Mike Smith, in a match designed to tune up the English players for the forthcoming first Test; I remember Geoff Boycott in particular was looking for a long innings after problems of adapting to South African conditions. John Price, the Middlesex fast bowler, was another playing for a Test place. Our labelling as 'Colts' was something of a misnomer, captained as we were by Peter van der Merwe and with experienced bowlers like Botten and Mike Macaulay. Neil Rosendorff and myself were the only representatives from the Nuffield tour, though of course some, like Prockie, were still behind their school desks.

Ted Dexter lost the toss, so we batted; my turn came after Price had forced Ian Fullerton to hit his own wicket and van der Merwe was caught behind by John Murray. I did not actually shake when I walked to the wicket, but I was no nerveless novice. The presence of Dennis Gamsy at the other end had some calming effect, but not quite as much as the relief of my initial runs in first-class cricket, a hook for 2 off Dexter which would have been worth double if Geoff Boycott had not stretched out his foot on the long-leg boundary.

Willowmoore Park in Benoni is a small ground with a benign wicket and there are much worse places to begin a career. I settled in to bat with the same attitude I would have applied to a club game, a contrast I'm sure to the beliefs of the seasoned pros I was facing; I picked the Sussex medium-pacer Ian Thomson off my legs for six and then set about Fred Titmus with the sweep— all this before lunch on the first day! In schoolboy cricket no spinners could make the ball drift in the air so I gaily lapped Fred several times, not realising that missing his 'floater' would bring the most almighty shout for lbw. I can still hear his groans of disbelief.

Some of the gloss disappeared when Dennis was run out after a mix-up between us, but when I swung once too often at Titmus and was stumped for 63 I was very pleased with the end product. Neil Rosendorff did even better with 89 and we finished with 398, mainly because the tourists had fielded as though the ball was charged with electricity. The game took a bizarre turn on the final day, when our side disappeared with the rapidity of the characters in 'Ten Little Indians'. Rosendorff, Macaulay, Botten and Tony Tillim suffered injuries, while Lorrie Wilmot contracted chickenpox, which also affected me after I had batted for not very many in the second innings. As we recuperated the following day, Mike Smith ordered extra fielding practice for the entire MCC party.

They provided altogether much sharper opposition when I played for Natal against them a fortnight later and we were beaten by 10 wickets. I missed out in our large first innings having a big swing at Cartwright and holing out to Bob Barber for 15; Derek Varnals top-scored with 111 out of 360 for 9 declared. But this time they batted like an international side with Dexter, Parfitt and Parks all passing 50, and David Brown, the night-watchman, hitting 69 in 105 minutes to add to our frustrations.

At the time Natal could field an extremely strong side, and they had won the Currie Cup with a certain inevitability for the previous four seasons. On this match the first five in the order, McGlew, Goddard, Varnals, McLean and Carlstein, were current internationals; the next five, myself, Dumbrill, Gamsy, Crookes and Trimborn, would all play for South Africa; while John Cole would certainly have represented his country had his sense of tact matched his highly-respected bowling. Yet, on a day of high humidity when the ball swung and seamed to an enormous extent, the MCC shot out this distinguished line-up in our second innings for 102.

I survived to make 29, though there were a number of occasions when I was so deceived by the late movement that I missed the ball by a foot. In the end David Allen, who finished with 4 for 12 in 15·3 overs, had me lbw, but I must have impressed him

along the way because within a few months he was to be responsible for another twist in my career.

He and David Brown were the only two tourists that I really
got to know; Brownie, big and amiable, really impressed me at
the time, his sociability more apparent because of the reluctance
of the remainder of the team to stay behind at the close of play to
share a drink. In South Africa and Australia the cricket isn't
complete without a crate of beer in the dressing-room and a chat
with the opposition. Having had ten years of county cricket I can
now understand the English attitude; cricket becomes a job, and
when it comes to knocking-off time in any walk of life the em-
ployee tends to leave his place of employment as soon as possible.

England won the series by virtue of a solitary victory at Durban,
in the first Test. But before the last game of the rubber the MCC
met a South African Invitation XI at Newlands in a four-day
match which to all intents and purposes was a trial for several
young players for the 1965 tour of England. I had already taken
part in a South v North trial earlier in the season with limited
opportunity. Now, before I had even established myself in my
provincial side, the press, with characteristic exaggeration, were
calling for my inclusion.

In the end my youth betrayed me. My 25 in the first innings
provided a reasonable advertisement for my claims; while Colin
Bland, in the middle of a golden dream run, played immaculately
for 116 and Gamsy, van der Merwe, Botten and Muzzell all
passed 50. In the second innings, though, I ran down the wicket
to the last ball before tea and was stumped; the selectors were
rather less than impressed.

The party to tour England was duly announced without the
name of B. A. Richards, but David Allen ensured that the insurance office would have to find another filing-clerk for the winter.
Before the MCC departed he took me aside and asked me if I
would like to have a summer with Gloucestershire if it could be
arranged; Prockie, he told me, had been interested in a similar
suggestion.

Agreeing to the proposal was hardly an irrevocable decision;
nevertheless it had its complexities. I had never considered playing
cricket for a living, and my parents were far from convinced that
it was suitable for their only son. At that time there was no prece-

dent of South Africans dotted around county cricket, as there is in the seventies. Roy McLean, Jackie McGlew and Trevor Goddard had all developed international careers from an amateur base at home; none of them had tried their hand at the full-time game.

The South Africans who were there fell into two categories; the lesser lights like Stuart Leary, who was pursuing a soccer career anyway, and whose cricket exploits received no coverage at home; or university Blues like Ray White, who joined a county during the vacation. For Prockie and me a season with a county, even though we were not qualified for the championship, would be an innovatory step.

In the end my choice boiled down to a simple decision—Gloucestershire or the insurance business; at nineteen years of age there was only one winner. Prockie and I accepted a deal in which we paid our fares, though the county later refunded us £50 each, and they gave us a weekly wage in the region of £15. Three pounds of that gave us bed and breakfast in a shared room of simple comfort in Bristol.

Those who heard my views on county cricket ten years later would have guffawed at the sheer enthusiasm we brought to our new life. Graham Wiltshire, who looked after the 2nd XI, collected us at Heathrow at ten o'clock on the evening of our arrival. By the time we had made the pre-motorway journey to Bristol and been introduced into our accommodation it was approaching four the following morning. But by half past ten we were at the ground ready to make our débuts in the 2nd XI.

That match remains a haze in my memory except that we managed little more than staying awake throughout. Warwickshire 2nd XI provided the opposition, and I do recall Eddie Hemmings bowling to me; in those days he was a carbon copy of Tom Cartwright at medium pace. This regular supply of professional opposition played an important role in the sharpening of skills for the years that lay ahead.

Both of us still approached our cricket with a dedication that I'm sure many of the Gloucestershire players saw as naïve. Even when there were no matches we went to the nets every day, practising harder than any of the other lads. We were never discouraged by the economic necessities of a county club which cut off the hot water supply when the first team played away and only the second team were using the nets. More than any experience on the field, I vividly recall the agony of those cold showers after a long work-out on a freezing May morning in Bristol.

At weekends, too, we would always volunteer for duty in matches for the International Cavaliers, or any benefit or charity occasion which needed numbers. The Bristol area certainly provided few distractions, but neither of us could play enough cricket.

The boys in the 2nd XI gave us a very warm welcome, as indeed did the county generally. Terry Riley, who had played a little first-class cricket with Warwickshire, was trying his luck with Gloucestershire at the time; he used to drive us in his Mini to away games like Evel Knievel on four wheels. Mike Bissex, who never quite fulfilled his promise, became a good friend, while Bob Etheridge and Martin Ashenden set up much of the dressing-room humour. Bob's party trick on away trips was to listen for the lady who brought the morning tea, sprawl out naked on top of his bed, feign sleep and wait for the reaction. Some didn't bat an eyelid, while others jumped out of their skins!

The bare statistics of that summer only partly explain its benefit. In competitive 2nd XI games I scored 632 runs, averaged 30·09, and took 29 wickets at just over 13 runs each—funnily enough finishing below Prockie in the batting averages, but above him in bowling. Taking my off-spinners very seriously, I even managed 4 for 5 in one game against Sussex. Most valuable of all was the day-to-day involvement with professional cricket, which I think gave me ever-increasing confidence in my abilities, even though at the time my ultimate ambition still lay in South Africa.

That ambition grew after the one first-class match of our stay in England. Though not qualified for the county championship, Prockie and I were both selected to face the South African tourists at Bristol. Rain restricted the game to the first day, but the match lasted long enough for both of us. John Mortimore won the toss and batted against a South African attack that was missing only Peter Pollock.

After the innings had stumbled along for an hour and a half we found ourselves at the wicket together, with Ron Nicholls, Syd Russell, Dave Brown and Mike Bissex back in the pavilion. Gloucestershire were 62 for 4 when Prockie came to the wicket for his first innings in first-class cricket. In the next hour and a half we put on 116.

Mike, particularly, responded to the opportunity of catching the eye of those who could influence our destinies at home. He cracked 14 fours in a splendid 69, heralded, on a par with a century from Brian Close for Yorkshire, as the best innings played against the tourists thus far. I found it more difficult, particularly against Harry Bromfield, who came within a whisker of bowling me twice in one over, and finally I was dropped at slip off Dumbrill. But in making 59 I felt I had passed another searching examination, and both of us secretly enjoyed the favourable comparisons drawn between our work and the form of our fellow countrymen so far on the tour.

We were, of course, also delighted to have made something of a splash for the county who had given us a chance, though in making an impact on the match we put them in an awkward position. The secretary's office was besieged with letters from supporters entreating the club to keep us on the staff, but though Jack Clarke, the chairman, and Richard McCrudden, the secretary, came up with generous offers which included off-the-field jobs, they were always on to a loser. To qualify we would have had to spend the full winter in England, which would prevent any Currie Cup cricket. Though flattered by the attention, I had no doubts. The ladders I wanted to climb belonged in Natal.

I returned to Durban in September after watching the rain at the Oval ensure South Africa's 1–0 victory in the three-match Test series. Gloucestershire had to have my final decision by November. I formally declined, with grateful thanks for a rewarding and hospitable season. It would take a change of qualification rules to bring about a change of heart. Only then would I finally recognise myself as a professional cricketer. Meanwhile, the insurance office and cricket with Natal beckoned, not necessarily in that order!

Chapter 6

Kicking Away my Chances

Apart from one hopeless attempt at cheating at school, the first twenty years of my life had been as controversial as a Julie Andrews movie. Within two months of returning from Bristol I found myself the centre of an on-the-field furore. Not much more than a year later an off-the-field episode was to cost me the opportunity of beginning my Test career four years before it finally and briefly flowered.

In the first incident I was an innocent victim; in the second not so—but that comes later. The benefits my batting had derived from my experiences against professionals showed immediately on my return home. In my first club outing, I rattled up 195 against Jackie McGlew's Old Collegians; and two more club hundreds, one in a floodlit match where they used a white ball, earned me the No. 3 spot in Natal's strong Currie Cup line-up. Technically I had not changed, but my attitude had matured. The schoolboy sense of apology for my ability had been hardened in the county dressing-rooms into a belief that I deserved my place out there in the middle.

I took my good form into the first Currie Cup match in the 1965–66 season against Rhodesia, reaching 68, a career best, before Goofy Lawrence dived to catch me at slip off Eddie Parker. More important to me was the fluency I managed, particularly against the leg-spin of Jackie du Preez, whom I drove for half a dozen boundaries. This was another boost to my confidence, particularly as I was being entrusted with the position in an order which had quality players like McGlew and Goddard in front of me and

Berry Versfeld, Roy McLean, Lee Irvine, Prockie and Dennis Gamsy to follow.

I kept my role in the following match against Natal, and then I ran into trouble in Port Elizabeth when we travelled to play Eastern Province. One of the early lessons I had learned, to my own amazement, was that several of the province teams would break the rules of the game by furtively applying lip-ice to the ball when they were fielding to increase the shine. Natal were no exception.

The accusations by the Indian Test team, subsequently proved to be without foundation, against England's John Lever in 1977 might have shocked purists who follow the game. From my experience tampering with the ball has gone on for a long time. At Port Elizabeth one of our players, with a reputation within South African cricket as a paragon of virtue, rubbed a large amount of lip-ice on the ball and tossed it to me. Only then did the umpire, Roley Stead, ask for an inspection. When he saw what had been applied he immediately assumed I was responsible for the application. At first I felt sure he was going to send me off the field, which would have caused a sensation amongst our most conservative cricket authorities and public. In the end he told me that I was a 'naughty boy' and wiped the ball on the grass; we resumed play and no official report was made. The newspapers did pick up the story, but I was not named. The actual guilty party, who has since retired, still retains his reputation as a pillar of sportsmanship.

My batting did not suffer from the rebuke. Chasing 210 in 187 minutes to win the game, I slogged 77, a new high, to put us within reach before I was adjudged lbw to Peter Pollock, a decision so diabolically bad that Peter and I still laugh about it. You might be forgiven for thinking that Roley Stead was punishing me for the doctored ball, but it was the other umpire, Cyril Millar, a really nice guy, in his last provincial match, who stunned Pollock and myself by raising his finger.

That match finished in a draw, but with a late run Natal won the Currie Cup when we beat Eastern Province in the return match, our last of the season, at Durban. My 61 in the second innings—a typical end to a run of scores around that mark—played its part, but the game's plot wove a final twist to provide a fairytale finish. Trevor Goddard had announced his retirement, but he seemed certain to be left with a disappointing memento when Eastern Province stood at 158 for 2, chasing 268, with Eddie Barlow on 106 and Graeme Pollock as his partner.

Goddard took an opposite view of the situation. Coming on at the City end, he immediately bowled Barlow at the start of a spell of 6 for 27 in one ball under 8 overs. What a perfect last exit—but this great all-rounder simply could not turn his back on the game he loved. Sinatra-like, he revoked the decision to quit and was still playing for his country almost four years later. We nicknamed him 'Rivers' after 'Ol' Man River', because he just kept rolling along.

I devoured the season like a good meal, but I knew that my appetite would not be satisfied until I had sampled the taste of Test cricket. The Australians under Bobby Simpson were scheduled for five Tests in the 1966–67 season. I could hardly wait for the months to pass before I had another opportunity to stake my claim to play against them.

Some of the waiting was eased by my third visit to England in four years. Wilfred Isaacs' private touring side comprised many senior players such as Hugh Tayfield, Roy McLean, Jackie McGlew, Neil Adcock and Paul Winslow; there was also room for Prockie, Lee Irvine and myself. This is an appropriate place for a word of tribute to Wilfred, a big man in every sense of the word, whose sheer enthusiasm has contributed greatly to South African cricket. He'd be the first to admit his shortcomings as a player, though he turned out four or five times on the trip, always making o until we finally persuaded the opposition to give him one to get off the mark. Even that was not easy for him.

Willie had been a fighter pilot in the war, and he'd organised this jaunt against county 2nd XIs plus a 'test' match in Holland, using his fighting spirit to badger companies for sponsorship. None of us received any payment, but all our expenses were met. Despite a number of social distractions I maintained reasonable form, but in retrospect I think a steady 46 not out against Hampshire 2nd XI at Bournemouth might have left the deepest imprint.

When the official tour finished, Mike, Lee and myself—with the security of our return ticket in our pockets—opted to stay on for a holiday. I've seen tramps with better resources than us, though.

We billeted ourselves in a vile boarding-house in Earl's Court and just about survived on the £2 a night we earned mopping out the Overseas Visitors Club.

But for a few days a chance meeting improved our lifestyles. We had gone to the Oval to see the first day of England versus West Indies only to find the 10s admission charge far beyond our means. We were about to slink back to Earl's Court when Geoff Howard, the Surrey secretary, recognised Prockie and me from the schoolboy tour. Would we like a job? Terrific. How about clearing up the ground at the close of play? A pause for thought and a quick evaluation of the debris left by 20,000 people. No thank you, we're desperate, but not that desperate. What about sweeping out the dressing-rooms? Yes, please!

So that was how three young South Africans found themselves attending to the whims of the West Indians. I can't imagine what my father thought when I wrote home, but I know the irony appealed to a lot of people. Funnily enough, none of the players I subsequently appeared with in the Rest of the World side in 1970, like Rohan Kanhai, Gary Sobers and Lance Gibbs, could remember us. I'll never forget big Wes Hall walking up to me with his pads and saying 'Give them a big clean, boy, I've got to make the runs today.' A free view of a Test Match and an income supplemented by a considerable haul of left-over cigarette packets and bottles of spirits made it a wonderful few days.

We flew back, not to Johannesburg, but to Rhodesia where we were scheduled to participate in an invitation match to celebrate the seventy-fifth anniversary of the Salisbury Cricket Club, Tony Pithey's XI versus Jackie McGlew's XI.

Many South Africans remember the day, Saturday 10th September 1966, the funeral of Dr Verwoerd, the assassinated Prime Minister; Jackie McGlew, in fact, chose as a mark of respect to remain in his hotel room until the funeral was over. I would be less than human if I didn't also remember it for my first hundred in senior cricket, 126 in 112 minutes for Pithey's XI, even though the three-day match was classified as non-first-class. Ray White followed up with a ton in 85 minutes, which may have inspired his devilry on the flight back to Johannesburg.

Ray was a notorious practical joker: he once tricked Lee into making the half-hour drive to the Wanderers ground three times in one day and each time changing for a photographer who, of course, never materialised. But, encouraged by Tiger Lance, he overstepped the mark on the plane. Somehow he stole three already completed customs forms. On mine he wrote that I had ten ounces of marijuana to declare; Prockie's revamped declaration suddenly revealed a 'Luger and ten rounds of ammunition to assassinate the Prime Minister'; flick-knives and other offensive weapons mysteriously appeared on Chris Wilkins' form.

Of course Mike and I never cast a second glance at our documents when we approached the customs officers. Ray must have been in convulsions as we were herded off to be fully searched despite our protests, though Chris discovered the alterations on his form and hastily wrote out a new one. In fact, the joke went too far. Only a couple of weeks after a real assassination you could expect an edgy reaction to a 'Luger and ten rounds of ammunition'. Drugs in the South Africa of 1966 were barely less subversive. We were held so long that we missed our connection to Durban, finally arriving several hours late, to the annoyance of both sets of parents, who had dutifully waited. Ray later phoned and apologised.

Despite the luxury—the Rhodesia trip excepted—of jetting around the world in the manner of the gossip columnists' most elegant socialites, the hard reality of my existence still remained in the insurance office. For all the fun I had with entertaining work-mates like Jake Clements, Tony Stalker and Angus Hutchinson, my income remained rock-bottom. Though I could keep noughts off the scoreboard, I couldn't find any way to add them to my pay checks.

Salvation appeared, however, in the form of a lucrative offer from Pretoria: a promotion in insurance, supplemented by coaching work, as long as I switched my Currie Cup allegiance to Orange Free State. In truth I never really fancied the move, with its switch to 'B' section cricket, but I was happy to publicise the offer simply as a means of obtaining better prospects in Durban. I was delighted to read headlines like 'Natal may lose Richards', under which the story included remarks about 'the uncertainty of my future'.

Just when it looked as though I might have to give Pretoria serious consideration, Mike Beare, a well known Durban businessman, became my benefactor. Ostensibly I was to sell furniture for him, though he gave me time to coach in the schools. I hope I coached well, because my attempts at persuading customers to buy furniture hardly justified the 150 rand he paid me each week— a rise of almost 100 per cent.

This settlement of my immediate future now allowed total concentration on making sufficient runs to challenge for a Test spot against Australia. I started the Currie Cup in Kamikaze fashion, running myself out for o twice in three innings. In our first innings against Eastern Province at Kingsmead, there were more ducks than in a poultry shop when Lee, Berry Versfeld and Dennis Gamsy also failed to score.

In a rearguard action in the second innings Alan Hector, a very underrated bowler of big inswingers, had me lbw for 96, a boundary away from that elusive first hundred. Then I ran myself out in the first innings against Transvaal.

Nevertheless, I impressed the selectors sufficiently to be included in a South African XI to play the Australians in East London. There, in the space of a couple of days, I built a tremendous opportunity to represent my country and then demolished my chances for the season. The wind gusted around the Jan Smuts ground when Trevor Goddard, back after his retirement, beat Bobby Simpson in the toss and opened our innings with Berry Versfeld. I came in, now a recognised No. 3, at 95 for 1, when Simpson himself had Goddard caught by Ian Chappell. At 245 for 2, I took a couple of paces down the wicket to Tom Veivers, the off-spinner, and drove him to the extra-cover boundary to finally pass the three-figure mark in first-class cricket.

Describing one's own performances is taxing to the modesty, but I can take blushing refuge behind a quote from Richie Benaud's report of that innings: 'Eleven Australian cricketers saw a new Test star born yesterday when 21-year-old Barry Richards carved a scintillating 107 off them. . . . He exhibited a cast-iron defence and glorious attacking strokes to all parts of the field in this two-and-a-half-hour stay.' I apologise to Richie now, because I ruined that particular forecast, for that season anyway, before the match had finished.

My downfall took place at the King's Hotel in town. Someone came to the match and issued us with a general invitation to attend a cabaret that evening. As I have mentioned earlier, it is the custom amongst Australian and South African cricketers to share a drink in the dressing-room after play. That night was no exception, and several measures had been downed by the time a group of us moved on to sample the hospitality of the King's Hotel.

Unfortunately none was forthcoming. The gentleman who had asked us was nowhere to be seen, nor had he told anyone to expect us. If the door was not actually slammed in our faces, the effect was the same. Even when Chris Wilkins, our twelfth man, arrived with his wife and tried to explain in less demonstrative terms that indeed we had all been invited, he received the same unbending refusal from the doorman. My temper began to burn on a short fuse.

Most of the players finally saw the futility of further discussion and drifted away, leaving only Acky, Prockie, Chris Wilkins and his poor wife and myself to continue what had begun as a debate and was developing into a scuffle. When even I realised that there was no way we would be seeing the cabaret that evening, I just had to vent my frustration in one final gesture. Alongside the outdoor swimming-pool stood a tall vase some four feet high. In my anger I kicked out at it and to my own surprise saw it tumble like a pin struck by a bowling ball. Contrary to later rumours, the vase itself did not fall in the water, but several sprinklings of earth did drop into the pool.

Before I could even savour my vengeance, the bouncer had whisked me into the manager's office, both of them determined to turn me over to the police. Prockie prevented that by grabbing the first person he recognised to come to my rescue; this was Derek Dowling, a South African selector. I'm not blaming Mike. But for him I could have spent the night in gaol and found myself in deeper trouble. Derek, who came from Natal, smoothed over my immediate problems by agreeing to cover the damages; in fact the cost of draining the pool came to no more than a few rand. But he naturally felt obliged to report the matter to his fellow selectors, and though he disagrees, I am sure I had literally kicked away that season's chance of Test cricket.

The message was patently clear the next morning. I had begun to pad up for the second innings when Trevor Goddard sidled over and in a rather embarrassed manner told me that I would be batting lower down the order. He muttered unconvincingly that it was because I had made my hundred in the first knock and that he wanted to give others an opportunity. In fact, I batted down at No. 8, where I was 12 not out at the declaration. In the fourth innings the ball turned and we were comfortable winners with 190 runs.

I hoped all would be forgotten when I performed reasonably well for Natal against the Aussies. At the end of the first day I raced to 38 in even time only to be caught at slip off McKenzie, first or second ball the next morning. In the second innings I grafted for almost four hours for 75, vainly trying to save the game. Later in the season I hit 88 and 65, opening for the first time, for another South African Invitation XI, finishing with 385 runs at an average of 77 from six first-class innings against the tourists. On the field I had more than established my claim, but the selectors—notably, I felt, Arthur Coy, a former chairman of the South African Cricket Association who had been in East London at the time of the incident at the swimming-pool—remained unforgiving. Had all things been equal, I still feel sure I would have been picked for the third Test. Ali Bacher was having a poor time at No. 3. I had struck a rich vein for Natal, and the game was at Kingsmead. But Ali was retained and Prockie, who had been twelfth man for the first two Tests, was awarded his first cap. I helped him celebrate—a riotous drunken party—but inside the disappointment hurt bitterly.

Bacher made runs in both innings of that match, cementing his place for the rest of the series. Just how much I had upset the apple-cart became clear when Hylton was selected as twelfth man in front of me for the fourth Test, though my consolation prize came in the final match of the rubber as twelfth man at Port Elizabeth. I did actually take the field for the first time in a Test Match in a brief, inglorious stint as a substitute fielder. My one contact with the ball ended in a wild throw over the wicket-keeper's head. For the rest it was the usual chores, especially that of forging some of the other players' signatures on the numerous bats that had to be autographed!

It had been an exciting series to miss. South Africa's win in the first Test had been our first-ever at home against Australia, thanks to a marvellous second-innings hundred from Denis Lindsay. For the team it was the first of three victories, for Lindsay the first of three centuries; in a tremendous personal triumph he finished with 606 runs plus 24 catches behind the wicket. Australia had evened the count by winning the second Test at Cape Town, even though Graeme Pollock had fought tooth and nail while making 209 in the second innings. It was the only success for Bobby Simpson's side, who would have been beaten 4–1 but for rain. Under the inspiring leadership of Peter van der Merwe, Trevor Goddard's left-arm medium-pace bowling frequently frustrated the Australians and he claimed 26 wickets in the rubber.

Though the affair had been entirely of my own making, I did feel slighted, especially as no official rebuke from the Board was ever delivered. I leaned heavily on my father's philosophy that you have to look after yourself in a tough world, and I became more determined to reach my goals.

I spent the South African winter building up my fitness, though I could no longer play rugby because of a weakness in my ankles which has plagued me since school. Even now my feet throb after a long period of exercise, which partly explains why I worked very hard to become a proficient slip fielder. Instead, squash became a regular pastime, and I developed sufficiently to represent Durban. I also took advantage of Mike Beare's generous hours of employment to join a lunchtime runners' club where a large number of working chaps with athletic ambitions collected every day at a local sports ground. The communal spirit stimulated me to participate because I have never had the willpower to train on my own. Running at midday and squash in the evening brought me to the 1967–68 season in the peak of condition.

I reaped the benefit immediately. I might have reached my first Currie Cup hundred in the first innings of the season, against Eastern Province at Port Elizabeth, but for a horrendous mix-up with Prockie which saw me run out for 78. In the second innings we were batting again together as I cautiously approached the figure for the second time in the match. On 99 he called for a sharp single designed to give me my hundred, only this time he couldn't make his ground. Still one short, I drove the next ball I faced, from Peter Pollock, to Peter Fenix at cover who dropped the catch. Eventually I obtained that precious run and finished with 135, and a week later, exactly a year after my 107 against the Australians, I scored 123 against North-Eastern Transvaal. Other hundreds came against Transvaal at Durban, 146, and then 114 in the second innings against them at the Wanderers in a remarkable match, after I had been out to the first ball of our first innings. Eddie Barlow bowled a loosener, short and wide, and I slashed it straight to Ali Bacher at slip. I faced the 'king pair' the same day as we followed on, and Eddie really turned the psychological screw. As I reached the middle Ali was chatting in mid-wicket, but in a stage whisper you could have heard in the dressing-room, Eddie told him, 'Get in the slips. He's on a pair, you'll probably get a catch.' This time I hit his first ball for four.

We made 277 in the second innings, leaving Transvaal plenty of time to make just 58 to win. But when they were a single run from victory, the heavens opened. Not just rain, but thunder, lightning, hail, the lot. We could not have prayed for more. Of course all the Natal side wanted to run for cover, and I'm sure no more play would have been possible. The umpires decreed that one more ball should be bowled.

If we stopped a run, instead of certain defeat the game would be drawn. Conscious of the fact that a leg-bye might be a likely route to a Transvaal victory, Berry Versfeld, who had succeeded Jackie McGlew as Natal's captain, moved an extra fielder just behind square-leg to counter that possibility. Mike Procter then raced through the downpour to bowl the final ball to Eddie Barlow, the thunder and hail emphasising the drama. Barlow aimed an almighty slog, and was bowled, but he was one of four men on the field who realised that Transvaal in fact had won. The fielder Berry had placed so carefully had been the third behind the wicket on the leg side; therefore Prockie's delivery was a no-ball. This had not escaped the attention of either umpire, nor of Lee Irvine down at long-leg, who had yelled for Mike not to bowl. Unfortunately, the storm drowned his shouts, but though I was livid at the time justice was done because we had been outplayed throughout the match.

In all it was a memorable season, considering there were no Tests to provide extra gloss. During it, news came from England that was to shape my life. The English cricket authorities had relented on overseas players; one per county would be given immediate registration for the 1968 county championship season. Gloucestershire were one of the first to take advantage; with a decision to make between the two green South Africans whom they had wanted two years earlier, they opted for Prockie. Apart from fitness worries, he has given them no cause to regret their choice.

He had received and accepted his offer long before I entered the marketplace. Then Sussex made a written approach and Hampshire a direct phone call. That in itself never produced a dilemma. Hampshire's offer almost doubled Sussex's. As in 1965, the question still remained. Was professional cricket the right choice for my career? My parents still cherished the dream that I would make my mark in more socially acceptable spheres; all sportsmen in South Africa, remember, were supposed to play for the love of the game. I countered that, at twenty-two, I had neither foot on any ladder to money and status, for all the benevolence of Mike Beare. If I had the security of a university education with all the attendant prospects, I might have settled for a comfortable existence at home. Of course I was excited when I accepted Hampshire's offer of a three-year contract, but in effect there was little alternative. At least the boat sailed straight to Southampton.

Chapter 7

Hampshire

Martin Harrison now lives in Australia, but he is as unlikely as I am to forget the English summer of 1968. For both of us it began amid much intense, but still good-natured argument about the politics of South Africa. It ended with the announcement on September 17th that the South African government would not accept Basil D'Oliveira as a member of the MCC party to tour my country in the 1968–69 season.

I had arrived in England almost six months earlier, by courtesy of P & O Lines, for my first season of county cricket. My debates with Martin arose from being billeted in his family home. Martin's father Leo was, of course, a long-serving Hampshire wicket-keeper, later coach and now committee man. Both he and his wife Joan sometimes found it difficult to get to sleep because of the late-night banter between their liberal-thinking university under-graduate son and a South African who still held sufficient pride in his upbringing to accept the racial status quo.

Despite those late nights the Harrisons made me feel more than welcome—even to the extent of providing a temporary base for Penny when she joined me in April before we found a flat together in Westward Road, Southampton. Elsewhere my arrival pro-voked more tepid reactions. In the indoor nets, for example, the senior players sat like judge and jury watching 'Butch' White, Hampshire's fastest bowler, test me out with an assortment of hostility. Somehow my salary of £1,300 for that first season had become common knowledge, and certainly some more experienced members of the staff begrudged a better wage than their own being given to a twenty-two-year-old with no Test career—an understandable attitude in retrospect but one that made life difficult at the time.

Unwittingly I didn't help my own cause when I said in a television interview that my aim was to make 2,000 runs in the season. This was just an off-the-cuff remark based on my performance in South Africa; I had made around 700 runs in 15 innings there, so I figured that 40 innings in England would give me the 2,000 target. I didn't feel that I had to justify myself in terms of my salary; I simply wanted to establish a reputation which would finally force me into the Test side against England.

In some quarters, however, my comments were interpreted as those of a bragging upstart; somehow I became quoted as the player who expects to make a large number of runs rather than one who coveted that target as an 'ambition'. Among the first to throw this misinterpretation back in my face were several players from Sussex, the opponents in my first county championship match.

Throughout the six weeks since my arrival I had detected a build-up to this first challenge. Some of my team-mates were particularly anxious to see whether I was worth this prince's purse I was being paid. Though this was my fourth trip to England and I had spent much of the pre-season in the nets at the County Ground, by the standards I was about to be subjected to my ears were still wet when we made the journey to Hove.

Roy Marshall and I had discussed what number I should bat on several occasions; I held no strong views. Roy and Barry Reed were a settled opening pair, so I went down on the card as No. 4. At Hove I did not have to wait long to go in—and even less time before I was back in the hut.

John Snow had hardly time to lick his lips at an overseas player playing back on a seaming track before he knocked over my castle, fifth or sixth ball, without scoring. Word of my television interview had reached some of the close fielders though accuracy had been lost in the post. I trudged back to the pavilion with comments like '2,000 is a long way off', or 'Just another 2,000 to go', stinging my ears. Although I was still naïve I was also aware that some of my team-mates were hardly shedding tears at my downfall.

That very evening, in the Imperial Hotel in Brighton, I didn't help my cause. My partners in crime were Bob Cottam, and two of the lesser known players, Alan Castell and Keith Wheatley. Quite how the transition took place from a couple of sorrow-drowning drinks to a corridor chase armed with lavatory brushes, I will never quite understand. But my horseplay changed to pure anger when one of the spiky brushes caught me a direct blow in the eye. I chased Alan and Keith into their room, and when I met a locked door I lashed out in blind fury. The bottom panel disintegrated like paper.

To my surprise Hampshire officially showed no interest in the matter, except to ensure that part of my first much-envied pay packet covered the cost of repairs. I later discovered that the hotel manager was quite used to such a rumpus because a couple of years earlier Colin Ingleby-Mackenzie had wrought similar havoc on a door panel with a spear!

My vision seemingly unimpaired, I fared much better in the second innings, when we played out for a draw after losing 2 for 12. Despite some more verbal intimidation from Michael Buss, who was a fiery character in those days, I ended up with 53 not out, my wicket and some of my reputation intact. I was already benefiting from the sage advice of my captain, who had followed my first-innings failure with a lecture on the necessities of front-foot play against English seamers.

I had hardly time to savour the joy of my reasonable second showing before I made my first acquaintance with another of the bugbears of the county cricketer: a travel schedule that makes the East African Safari look like a Sunday afternoon cruise. The next match took place the following day at Harrogate against York-shire, some three hundred miles north of Brighton with all of London to circumnavigate. Since then England's motorways have been greatly improved, yet cricket's administrators, with the complexities of a multi-competition structure, have still managed to keep pace with the improved roads by devising even more nerve-shattering journeys.

We arrived at Harrogate at two o'clock in the morning, only to find that no one could get a nightcap; it was a temperance hotel. I did not lead the complaining; despite the high jinks in Brighton I now, as then, still prefer a soft drink to the occasional lager. Besides I had already discovered that my South African habit of buying a round did not fit into the lifestyle of certain county players. One or two had cultivated the art of fumbling for their change for so long that someone else picked up the bill. Even at this time I had noticed that my turn to pay came round much more frequently than that of some others.

There was to be nothing dry, however, about the summer. At Harrogate we were lucky to start at all; the wicket was wet at one end, where moisture had seeped under covers, and firm at the other; I had seen nothing like it before and Yorkshire, with Fred Trueman, Tony Nicholson, Ray Illingworth and Don Wilson, were perfectly equipped to make me struggle. In the event my third innings for Hampshire remains one of my most treasured. I battled my way to 70 out of a total of 122, this against bowlers whose names I held in awe. I could find no reply when Fred, in these miserable conditions, turned past me at the non-striker's end and grunted 'Ee, lad, bowling's not all beer and skittles.'

Those first few days provided a microcosm of the entire season, a patchwork of experiences, some stimulating, some aggravating, all memorable. Such is cricket's repetitive circuit that often reflection tricks the memory; the events of one season easily blend into those of another. Yet as in much of life, the first time remains crystal-clear.

At Harrogate, for example, Butch White, whom you could never really describe as nimble, raced twenty-five yards and then dived to catch Geoff Boycott off a top-edged skier. Although it was a brilliant catch Butch was less than pleased: his gear was completely caked because he slid another twenty yards on his backside on the muddy surface. As he picked himself up, he found his team-mates rolling with hysterical mirth.

This first road trip ended at Edgbaston where the weather relented just long enough for a spell of wide-eyed fielding when Rohan Kanhai was batting. The last time I had seen him I had been cleaning his pads as the Oval dressing-room attendant. I was also looking forward to my first look at Majid Khan, then Majid Jehangir, who was in the Glamorgan side in my home début match. Both of us betrayed our backgrounds on a typically English rain-affected wicket. I made 2 and 2; poor Majid suffered a pair.

I balanced my account with a 50 at Bournemouth against Middlesex, where yet again the elements interfered with play, and our next trip brought an early return to Bristol. No doubt the Gloucestershire committee watched the match with extra interest, since they had chosen Prockie in front of me. He did not let them down. With Gloucestershire 49 for 5 he and Mike Bissex pulled the innings together, Prockie scoring a brilliant 101. My contribution was 0 and 14, leaving me only with the satisfaction that Mike didn't get me out and that we won the match by 5 wickets; it was our first victory of the season, achieved on the back of Bob Cottam's 6 for 35 in their second innings.

Though I had not really been struggling, I had hardly set the South Coast alight, which may have been the reason Roy Marshall asked me if I'd fancy changing positions with him and opening the innings. Though my only real experience had been in the second South African Invitation XI match against the Australians, I was content to give it a try. I could not have made a better start.

Roy decided to conduct the experiment against Northamptonshire, a county at that time not overblessed with penetrative opening bowlers. In the first innings Barry Reed and I put on 182 and I finished with 130; in my second knock I was 104 not out, out of 154 for 1, when Roy declared on the final afternoon. In all fairness Northamptonshire were then bowling to help us declare, and even Hylton Ackerman was given an over. More because I did not know what to expect than out of courtesy to an old friend, I blocked it out. At the time, I felt that Roy's declaration, 240 in 160 minutes, was too steep, though I would not have dreamt of saying so. I would soon abandon the philanthropic notions of home for the practical views that county captains have to take.

If the two hundreds ensured me of an extended trial in my new role, they did not guarantee success. In the next game against Kent I spent a long time sitting in the bath smouldering after being adjudged lbw to John Dye for 4. Between curses I would stare at the bruise on my thigh where I had been hit, confirmation in my own mind that the ball would have passed over the stumps. A few years would pass before I could control my anger at getting out.

The match itself ended in the drabbest of draws because of a friction that had apparently existed for several years between Colin Cowdrey and Roy Marshall. Mindful that good declarations had rarely been set in this fixture, Cowdrey set nothing at all, batting on to the dissatisfaction of a Bank Holiday crowd and allowing John Shepherd to achieve a maiden first-class century against bowling which could hardly be described as testing.

Another draw came against Somerset where I fell to another left-arm opening bowler, Fred Rumsey, for 0, but I got back on the rails with 62 in the second innings. Bill Alley bowled me, probably making the old ball move off the wicket. He had me caught behind at Bath a couple of weeks later, too, after I was well set past 50; I would wager that delivery suddenly nipped off the seam as well!

Glamorgan beat us by an innings at Cardiff, where Majid unveiled his majesty with 91 on such a difficult wicket that Peter Walker and Tony Cordle bowled us out for 52. Then came victories at Bath and against Warwickshire at Basingstoke, where I claimed my third century of the summer. I remember Butch White telling us that one of Warwickshire's senior batsmen would hop with discomfort under a barrage of bouncers' Butch was rarely wrong and in 1968 he picked out Dennis Amiss's problems —though it would be five or six years before that weakness would be fully exposed by Lillee and Thomson, and Holding and Roberts.

In the dressing-room I continued to maintain a low profile, particularly as I could still not be sure how each of the team was reacting to my presence. In matters of tactics I simply sat and listened; I just felt that I had not sufficient know-how to make any positive comment. As far as Roy's leadership was concerned, I happily went along with it, content to watch and learn. One early difficulty was coming to terms with the comparatively leisurely pace at which the county game is played, for reasons of simple energy conservation. In South Africa, where games take place less frequently, every player is highly strung and totally involved in the match from the first ball to the last.

I was not afflicted by one problem which continues to strike down so many young English batsmen. It was typified by Lancashire's visit to Portsmouth in 1968, where Brian Statham took three quick wickets on his reputation alone. His mere presence in the opposing ranks unsettled the dressing-room before we started our innings. He must have been a great bowler, but then, at the end of his career, I played him as I found him and coped without undue difficulty until rain, inevitably, ended the match.

We did beat the weather and Leicestershire at Grace Road before coming across one of the worst wickets I have ever had the misfortune to bat on. The Gillingham pitch just lasted the length of the first innings of the match, which was Kent's; we had not lost a wicket in reply when Barry Reed played forward to a good-length delivery from Derek Underwood and the ball hit him on his cap. 'Deadly' Derek smiled in anticipation and took 11 wickets in the match, bowling Hampshire out in our second innings for 58. The ground was subsequently banned from first-class cricket.

On 12th July I passed 1,000 runs, fulfilling at least half of my target less than a fortnight after Rohan Kanhai and Roger Prideaux had been the first two county batsmen across that particular line. More pleasing, because of their rarity, were bowling figures of 21 overs, 12 maidens, 25 runs, 3 wickets to help overturn Essex at Bournemouth; it would have been 4 wickets, but as I trapped Keith Fletcher plumb in front I ran in front of the umpire and he had to give him not out.

By a quirk of the fixtures both sides then travelled to Westcliff for the return match. Another remarkable wicket, where Brian Taylor looked long and hard at green patches on a length, decided to bat and saw Essex tumbled out for 95. I actually took one ball from Derek Shackleton at slip after the movement off the pitch had been so extreme that it beat both batsman and wicket-keeper. Defending surely would only delay inevitable downfall, so I resolved to flail away for as long as I could.

I survived for over four and a half hours and ended with 176. My most successful tactic was to drive the spinners, Robin Hobbs and Ray East, over extra cover, which was quite foreign to English players who had been schooled to work every possible delivery on the leg side. Nowadays more batsmen have realised the relative safety of the shot. I have only played at Westcliff once since then, and I got a pair, the only one in my career; fate took its revenge for allowing me to play that one big innings on such a nasty wicket.

We duly completed a victory by an innings at Westcliff, and then beat Nottinghamshire at Worksop, where I played against

Gary Sobers for the first time. He didn't disappoint me, making an exhilarating 67 while the last innings of the match fell around him. At that time we took up the running for the championship, but we were to win only one more game. However our final position was fifth, which did represent a considerable improvement on the previous season.

My education continued. I had developed the habit of going down the wicket to medium-pace bowlers and in the short term it paid dividends. In that one other victory, against Sussex at Portsmouth, I scored 80-odd quickly in each innings by using this tactic against Tony Buss and Don Bates. I combined it with the bluff of feinting to advance and then being ready on the back foot to clout the ball over mid-wicket when the bowler dropped short as a response. In the right mood I would charge one delivery, feint the next two and then charge another.

But as I was to discover, word spreads quickly around the county circuit. Ken Higgs, then of Lancashire, was ready for me. His remedy was simple. When I went down the wicket he bowled the ball on the full straight at my head. I just hit the dirt and I would have been stumped if Farokh Engineer had not missed the wicket with his throw. I've batted against Ken many times since he returned to the game with Leicestershire and I don't think I've given him the charge since.

Revenge was nearly the theme for the Australians, against whom I had enjoyed myself so much in South Africa. They should have dismissed me for a pair at Southampton. Ian Chappell caught me at slip for 0 off Graham McKenzie at the start of the match, completing the catch between his knees after letting it slip through his hands. In the second innings I opened my score with an edge at catchable height which flew between Chappell and second slip.

Against Leicestershire I blotted my copybook when I edged John Pember to Ray Julian behind the wicket and did not walk for the only time in my career in England. The umpire gave me not out, and I just stood there looking embarrassed. I can only think that it was because I felt that such a bad ball, wide down the leg side, did not deserve a wicket. I tried to take my bat out of the way but I just made the faintest of contacts. I apologised to Maurice Hallam, their captain, after the day's play, which he accepted with a rebuke which was more a word of advice than one of warning. Ray Julian might have been less forgiving; he became an umpire and I'm sure he has enjoyed giving me out on several occasions since then.

These days the majority of English players still walk. Most Australians freely admit that they leave it to the umpire; the only time an Aussie walks is when his car runs out of petrol. Today the rewards for success are so much higher; sponsorship has saved the game, but with more at stake the ethics will inevitably change. Though I still choose to walk I can understand the niggling that has come into cricket; it is impossible to have the best of both worlds, and cricket would expire without the precious financial aid introduced by the commercial sponsors.

When I am bowling, of course, I take a different perspective, but no controversy arose when at the end of the 1968 season I somehow bowled out a star-studied line-up to bring Hampshire victory over a Rest of the World XI. Seymour Nurse, Clive Lloyd, Basil Butcher, Eddie Barlow, Saeed Ahmed, Graeme Pollock and Wes Hall all contrived to depart to my off-spin. The 7 for 63 has stood for ten years as my best performance with the ball, though in recent seasons I've rarely managed 7 wickets in a season.

I think, however, it was my batting they were after when the Rest of the World team recruited Roy Marshall and me to play for them in the next match of their tour at Canterbury against Kent. It was a crazy game. Hanif Mohammed captained our side and he put me in at No. 6 in the first innings, where I was promptly bowled by John Shepherd for 0. After Brian Luckhurst had set up a declaration for the county with a century in each innings, Hanif came over to me and said: 'They tell me you're opening batsman. You go in first instead of me.' He felt unwell, which hardly surprised any of us when we discovered he kept the heating full on in his hotel room with his bed swathed in blankets. 'It is the same temperature as my home,' he explained to those who had found saunas colder than the captain's chamber.

Kent lost the match because Eddie Barlow had a plane to catch; he and Graeme Pollock were flying to the Continent for a holiday at five o'clock that afternoon. Our opening partnership put on 225; Eddie's share was 153 in 145 minutes before the clock ticked

to the appointment hour and he offered up a stumping chance off
Stuart Leary, who also had me caught for 81.

The silly season continued when I returned to Hampshire for
the last home match of the season against Nottinghamshire. I had
scored 29 when I chased a wide delivery outside the off stump
from Carlton Forbes and got an inside edge. The ball flicked the
stumps and sped past Deryck Murray, the wicket-keeper, to the
boundary. I did a double-take when I noticed that the bails had not
fallen to the ground. In those days the Portsmouth ground,
which is serviced by the most enormous roller in county cricket,
produced a really hard wicket. Hammering in the stumps became
a prodigious feat and, once placed, it was as though they were set
in concrete. Though the stumps had been hit hard, there simply
had not been enough momentum to knock one out of a vertical
line sufficient to dislodge a bail.

New sets of stumps were produced, and nowadays the area
where the holes are made is watered to make the holding looser.
But all might have been forgotten if I had been dismissed shortly
after the incident. Instead I made 206, a batting best to follow the
bowling performance of the previous week. Mike Taylor, a
cricketer for whom I gained the greatest respect when he joined
Hampshire five years later, suffered most of all. A nagging medium-
pacer, he bowled me two very accurate maidens in his first spell;
then I began going down the wicket to him. Later he was to tell
me that no player had ever done that to him before.

During the course of the innings I passed 2,000 runs for the
season, but I resisted the temptation to send a cable to the Sussex
dressing-room informing them of the fact. In our last match at the
Oval, against Surrey, I reached 2,000 in the county championship.
I don't think that in doing so I killed off all the resentment within
the Hampshire camp. I have never done that entirely, but in the
first year in which cricket became a profession for me rather than
a pastime, I felt I had done my job.

Penny and I flew back home as soon as the season finished. With
the England touring side due for a five-Test series, I was almost
purring at the prospect. The South African press had already
written my praises with the gusto of scribes who had exhausted
their descriptions of McLean, McGlew and Goddard. I couldn't
wait to demonstrate what I had learnt in England.

In my youthfulness I failed to recognise the existence of a problem. I was too wrapped up in my own career. Of course, I had heard murmurings of adverse South African reaction to Basil D'Oliveira's presence in the England side. But it would all be sorted out. Politicians dramatised such situations, but they always found a solution. With or without D'Oliveira—and at that time, however naïve it may seem now, to me he was just another county cricketer—the tour would go on. As every cricket-lover now knows, I could not have been more wrong.

Chapter 8

First and Final Tests

To most South Africans a heavy cloud of suspicion hangs over the D'Oliveira affair. I am no exception. Even now, almost ten years later, the sequence of events remains amazing. Basil's fairytale recall to the English side for the fifth Test against Australia—he made 158 and took a vital wicket in the successful scramble for victory after rain had apparently saved the tourists—surely guaranteed his place on the tour. At the time I just could not understand how a player who is regarded as good enough to win a spot in the final Test of a series, and who plays a mammoth innings, cannot be worth a position in a party of sixteen. It defies cricketing logic.

The selectors' explanation took into account his relatively poor showing in the West Indies the previous winter; they also stated that they had regarded him purely as a batsman. The first point surely did not take into account Basil's experience of his native South Africa. The second left itself open to derision when D'Oliveira was seconded to the party as a replacement for Tom Cartwright, a specialist bowler.

Within twenty-four hours of D'Oliveira's recall Dr Vorster, the Prime Minister, announced rather pointedly in Bloemfontein, where cricket is not fanatically supported, that South Africa was not prepared to receive a team with 'certain political aims'. Though the MCC took another week to announce the formal cancellation, Test cricket between South Africa and England effectively ceased at that point.

Had Basil been among the original selection, that tour might not have taken place, but I'm sure I would have played Test cricket against England at a later date. Rugby, as I have mentioned earlier, provided a precedent for this when bans on Maoris and French coloureds were later lifted. Now, however, the English selectors' strange omission and recall gave the South African government the excuse they needed.

Both sets of cricket authorities were to blame. Though the political ramifications remain an untold story, I feel sure that the MCC were trying to protect South African cricket; after all in no way did the organising body, which I feel does a splendid job, want to be party to any severing of cricketing links.

From my experience I would be very surprised if the South African officials helped our cause. Their whole attitude has always been that of a poor relation; I have never met a South African cricket administrator with the authority to put over an idea of our domestic problems and points of view. This attitude—that South Africa was rather fortunate to be playing at such a level—reflected so often in our Test Match performances. Only when Eddie Barlow came on the scene was there a positive approach. He taught his and subsequent generations that we were 50 per cent of any game and we were going to play a full 50 per cent role.

The theme at the time was that politics should be kept out of sport. I'd certainly keep politics out of my life. At Hampshire I had enjoyed the company of Danny Livingstone, the batsman from Antigua, more than that of many of my colleagues; I'd got on well with Roy Marshall who, although he is white, is a West Indian; I had been thrilled to talk to Garfield Sobers and Rohan Kanhai when Hampshire played against them.

At 22, I just loved playing cricket. I looked to the game for my whole future, and in 1968 time was on my side. I had years of cricket ahead of me and I was utterly convinced that the cancellation of the tour was no more than a temporary setback. A total grasp of the situation was beyond me; I still could not comprehend the complexity of South Africa's problems. Disappointed, I certainly was; dejected I was not. I simply shifted my sights towards Australia's visit a year later.

Both the disrupted season at home and the 1969 English season were ways of consolidating my still unsatisfied ambition. I retained my new role as opener back in the Natal side, although I had expected that I would continue to go in at the fall of the first

1 (*above*) No shyness in front of the cameras—even at this age.

2 (*left*) On Durban's beach front when my only ambition was to become a lifeguard.

3 Natal Schools XI. Also in the back row Prockie, extreme left, and Lee Irvine, fourth from left.

4 Talking cricket bats with Prockie and Stuart Surridge at his factory during the 1963 South African Schoolboys tour.

5   Manager and mentor—Jackie McGlew in an advisory role at the Lord's nets during the 1963 tour.

6   Brought down to earth by Richie Benaud's flipper at the Oval in 1963.

7   A jubilant appeal for a stumping off Jackie McGlew during my early days as a wicket-keeper.

8   Prockie and Lee seem to be doing all the work during our spell as dressing-room attendants during the England versus West Indies Test at the Oval in 1966.

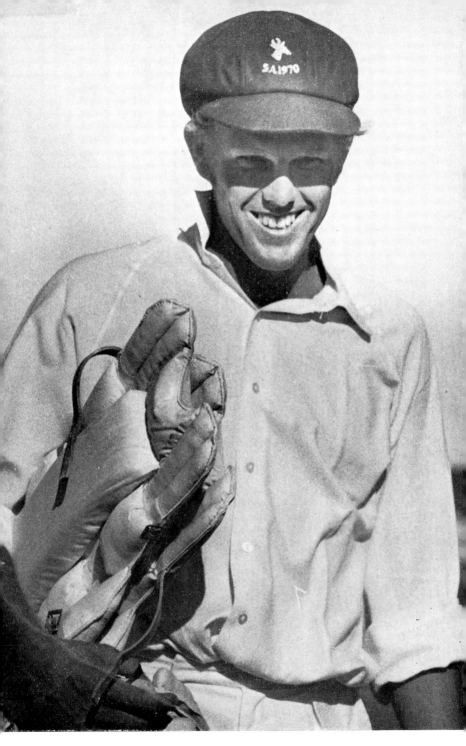

9   Wearing the prized cap at last—even in the nets during the 1970 series against Australia. (Photo: *Eastern Province Herald*)

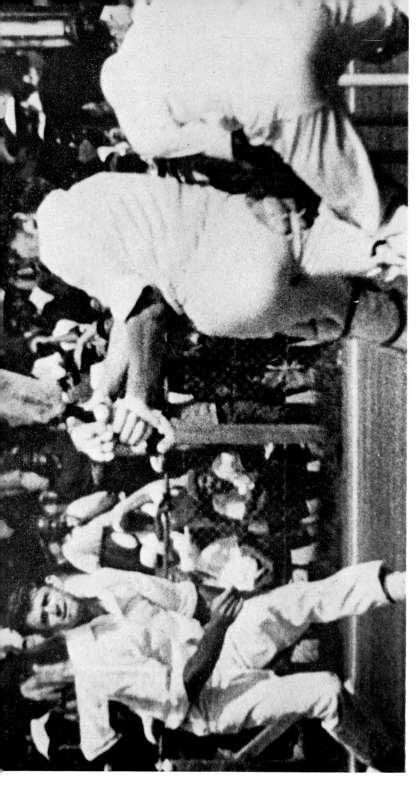

10 Against John Gleeson the only form of defence was attack during the 1970 series. (Photo: *Africamera*)

11   Rod Marsh can only watch as I collect four more off Dennis Lillee on my
way to 356 for South Australia against Western Australia in Perth in 1971.
(Photo: *Adelaide Advertiser*)

12 It doesn't all come naturally—lapping the Melbourne Cricket Ground in 1971 in the cause of peak fitness.

13 At the presentation of the Viscount Hampden Trophy at the end of the 1970-71 season—with Ian Chappell, John Causby, Eric Freeman, Greg Chappell and Neil Dansie.

14 On my way to a hundred for Hampshire against Lancashire in the 1972
Gillette Cup. Farokh Engineer behind the stumps. (Photo: *Pctrick Eagar*)

15　The happy captain with the Currie Cup—surrounded by those who made victory possible—Pat Trimborn, Bob Woolmer, Henry Fotheringham, Darryl Bestall, Vince van der Bijl (partly hidden), Aubrey Lilley and Pelham Henwood. (Photo: *The Star*, Johannesburg)

16　A coaching clinic in Soweto. South African Test players of the future? (Photo: *The Star*, Johannesburg)

17 Friend and Hampshire opening partner Gordon Greenidge. (Photo: *Patrick Eagar*)

18 Chewing gum for Gordon during a break in the slips where it was our hands which were sticky during Hampshire's championship success. (Photo: *Patrick Eagar*)

19 Hampshire's championship-winning squad 1973. *Back row:* Richard Lewis, Dave O'Sullivan, Mike Taylor, Tom Mottram, Bob Herman, Gordon Greenidge, Andy Murtagh, Trevor Jesty. *Front row:* David Turner, Peter Sainsbury, Richard Gilliat, Barry Richards, Bob Stephenson. (Photo: *Patrick Eagar*)

20   Prockie and me, old friends and rivals, Hampshire versus Gloucestershire at Bournemouth in 1973. (Photo: *Patrick Eagar*)

21   A happy reunion with the 1975 Australians at Southampton—Rod Marsh, Greg Chappell and Ross Edwards. (Photo: *Patrick Eagar*)

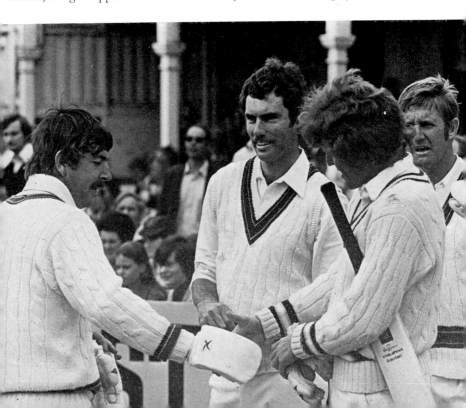

22 I wish I had a penny for every autograph I have signed. Trevor Jesty helps me do the honours on arriving to play Surrey at the Oval. (Photo: *Patrick Eagar*)

23 Training for the future? The enjoyment of broadcasting—on this occasion for Radio Victory in Portsmouth.

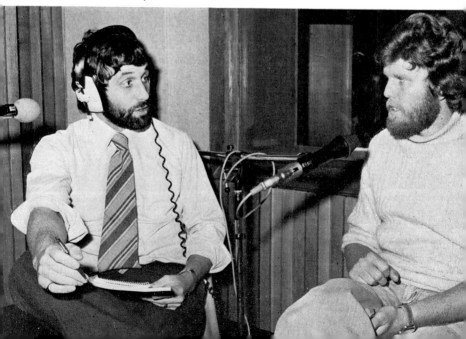

24 Felled—by the Australian fast bowler Alan Hurst during the third match of the series between the South African Invitation XI and the International Wanderers in 1976. (Photo: *The Daily News*, Durban)

25   Thank you for all the applause. (Photo: *Southern Evening Echo*)

wicket. Somehow it took me a long time to adjust to becoming an opener. I saw it as a blocker's role, because in those days the dour players went in first. Jackie McGlew, especially, and Trevor Goddard were hardly renowned for knocking the cover off the ball. Of course nowadays, with the likes of Gordon Greenidge and Majid Khan opening, it has all changed. Then, I saw myself as a cavalier being asked to graft.

Natal finished far behind Transvaal in the Currie Cup after a season of misfortune. Trevor Goddard and Berry Versfeld, both of whom captained the side, sustained injuries; Grayson Heath, who took over the leadership at the Wanderers, ended that game in hospital suffering from nervous exhaustion. Versfeld's injury—he was felled by a very fast bouncer from Peter Pollock—marked the beginning of the end of his career. He never truly recovered the form that made him a firm Test candidate; a real pity, because he had such a natural eye that he represented Natal at baseball, and actually travelled to the United States for a trial with the Pittsburgh Pirates.

Though I only recorded one century, I achieved the necessary consistency for an opening batsman, and apart from very odd occasions I have retained the spot. I still managed to land myself in trouble once during the season with my newly developed lack of diplomacy. In our first Currie match, against Rhodesia at Salisbury, I became agitated when Ray Gripper, an opener who was certainly no cavalier, held us up in the fourth innings; he had thwarted us before and I could see another frustrating performance from him. He had made 80 when I ran him out as he backed up too eagerly.

In such circumstances the accepted code of behaviour is a warning first. But my impatience and my pent-up will to win scattered convention to the winds. I ran in to bowl and saw him out of his ground. I knocked the bails off, appealed and, of course, the umpire had no option but to give him out. Even my teammates were embarrassed.

Injuries disrupted my return to England and I missed six county championship matches. The season wore a new look with the introduction of the John Player County League, as it was originally called; the 'Sunday Slog' became the dressing-room term of abuse for the 40-over competition. The players held mixed views; its popularity undoubtedly revived interest at the turn-stiles, but the crash-bash winning style was hardly cricket as we knew it. Moreover, it filled our one scheduled previous day of rest. I have been very successful on Sundays over the years, but to be honest I would rather have spent every one of those resting for the three-day competition. Though I have made several thousand John Player runs, I can hardly remember one innings in any detail.

But seven innings in 1970 I shall never forget. Unless there is a rapid change of political thinking, those seven knocks against Bill Lawry's Australians comprise my Test career. Again at the time, I had no conception of the barrier that was about to be dropped. Recognising my tendency to occasionally toss away my wicket in a moment of indiscretion, I am glad that I did myself justice. Even so, I should have made more runs.

I am not too modest to say that I did expect to be chosen for the series. After all I had been in Currie Cup cricket for six years, and I had enjoyed two prominent seasons with Hampshire. Moreover in Natal's four Currie Cup games before the first Test I had scored three centuries, the last of which was 169 against Rhodesia, when Arthur Short and I put on 258 for the first wicket. Despite my confidence, I still tingled with delight when I heard on the radio that I had been picked; after all the previous frustrations the announcement was very, very pleasing.

The Australians arrived with the highest reputation; they held the Ashes, the previous season they had comprehensively beaten the West Indies 3–1 and they flew in for a twelve-week tour, to the gratitude of every South African cricket lover, straight from another 3–1 series victory in India. Only later would the detrimental effects of the latter rubber become apparent.

Ian Chappell, Doug Walters, Keith Stackpole and Paul Sheahan had all made Test centuries against the Indians, and of course Bill Lawry himself was the most obdurate of opponents. Graham McKenzie and Alan Connolly would be a testing new-ball attack, supported by the off-spin of Ashley Mallett and the unusual skills of Johnnie Gleeson.

No magician could have come to South Africa with a greater aura of mystery than Gleeson. His secret lay in his unusual use of the middle finger, which he bent behind the ball as he held it; he could then flick this finger to either side to impart either off- or leg-spin. Unlike most spinners, he prefered to bowl with the wind. Many top-class batsmen had been unable to read him.

In his two first-class matches before the first Test Gleeson took 18 wickets. Naturally the Australians and the press began to build a psychological war, and if you believed all you read in those couple of weeks, walking on water was one of his lesser accomplishments. It annoyed me, and I told one reporter that, fine bowler though he was, he had no magical properties and that he was not unplayable. The headlines screamed out their messages to the effect that 'Richards says Gleeson is no bogey'. The Australians need no excuse to indulge in a verbal battering of a nervous batsman in his first Test: because of that article they were especially ready for me.

The series began at Cape Town. Ali Bacher, captaining his country for the first time, won the toss, as he was to do throughout the series. Prockie always reminds me how edgy I appeared to be before I went out to bat, but although the occasion did have its effect, I was not as nervous as Trevor Goddard, who was playing in his thirty-ninth Test. It obviously gets worse as you go along.

Against McKenzie and Connolly I began with immense care. It took me more than twenty minutes to get off the mark. My initial runs in Test cricket came from a square drive for four off Connolly, quickly followed by a huge sigh of relief. Trevor had made 16 out of 21 when Doug Walters, the first change, dismissed him. Ali Bacher and I then put on 75.

Ali's quickness into his stride provided a boost to my confidence. He was a very unorthodox player—any ball on the stumps would be hit through mid-wicket—but his chancy technique was supported by an excellent eye and a superb temperament. He regularly came down the wicket between overs offering words of encouragement, sensitive to the barrage of abuse the Australian fielders gave me. Paul Sheahan, in particular, snarled away, reminding me what I had said about Gleeson.

I did survive against the mystery man but not against Connolly, who bowled me off the inside edge for 29. I kicked myself, because I had done most of the hard work and reached a point where I should have gone on to a big score. Eddie Barlow, how-ever, did not miss out, batting for six hours for 127, and we totalled 382. His innings, though, marked the beginning of the bad feeling which remained throughout the series.

Off the very first ball of the second morning, umpire Billy Wade gave Eddie not out after the entire Australian side leapt in the air to appeal for a catch behind the wicket; Barlow had then scored 66. From then on the atmosphere on the field, sharpened by two or three other unfortunate decisions, bordered on hos-tility. Billy Wade, always 'Uncle Billy' to me, did not deserve to be at the centre of such a storm. A former Test player himself, he is as far from being a cheat as you could ever imagine. The Australians, who never walk themselves, could hardly expect Eddie to do the same when Billy, in complete honesty, gave him not out.

In fact in their dressing-room there were two schools of opinion: those who realised that bad decisions even themselves out and are a fact of cricket life at all levels; and some players who sincerely believed they were playing against thirteen men. Either way they allowed their morale to be lowered from this point only a few hours of play into the series.

In our 382, Gleeson, whom we had christened 'Heinz' because of his fifty-seven varieties, had bowled magnificently, but his final figures were 1 for 92 in 45 overs. He was to take 19 wickets in the series, but morally he had many more because none of our batsmen played him with any true certainty; his ill-luck struck even further at Australia's team spirit. Funnily enough, I only heard about his secret much later; the delivery that looked like a leg-break was an off-spinner, while the ball you thought must be an off-break was a leg-spinner. Once word got around, his mystery disappeared and he faded from the scene.

Australia's reply could not have been more sensational. In provincial matches leading up to the Test Bill Lawry had scored 86 not out, 157 not out, 9 not out and 43 not out, thirteen hours of unbeaten batting. Peter Pollock rapidly ended that run, bowling him round his legs for 2. The crowd's roar echoed from Table Mountain. Three balls later he gave Ian Chappell the welcome of a bouncer, but somehow Lee Irvine at leg-gully thrust up a hand to parry Chappell's hook. The ball lobbed gently to Graham

Chevalier at leg-slip, a desperately unlucky dismissal which set Ian off on a terribly bad patch throughout the series.

Australia never recovered from 5 for 2. Eddie Barlow, one of those cricketers, like Tony Greig, with a magic touch, caught Stackpole and Redpath at slip off Prockie. Only Doug Walters, with 73 out of their final total of 164, stayed a while, though as so often happens, he never really suggested permanence. He played several great shots but, as John Snow was to find out during the next England-Australia series, the bouncer unsettled him. Even on the slow wicket at Newlands he fashioned the periscope shot, ducking and leaving his bat above his head. But nothing ever worries Dougie, a really phlegmatic character, and he just smiled as the ball shot off to third man for a run.

In such a dominating position I naturally took the opportunity to take revenge on Paul Sheahan. He arrived with the reputation of an elegant front-foot player and I would shout at Prockie: 'Here comes the show pony. Let's see this big stylist driving when the ball's whistling around his ears.' All part of the game, and Paul and I would still share a drink at the end of the day's play.

With the ball starting to turn, Ali decided not to enforce the follow-on. By now I was much more relaxed, but after playing more strokes than in the first innings I again got out when well set. Brian Taber, standing up, caught me, once more off Connolly, for 32. In our haste to build on our lead several wickets fell in similar vein, and no declaration was necessary. Connolly's perseverance brought him 5 for 47 and we were all out for 232.

Though Australia could only hope for a draw, their second innings offered much more substance. But only Lawry with 83, and Redpath with 47 not out, threatened to deny us. To try to unsettle Redpath, Ali tossed the ball to me, and I should have had him out with my first delivery in Test cricket. There have been few longer hops bowled in such distinguished circumstances, and in time-honoured fashion Ian could not decide whether to hit it for four or six. Instead he pulled it straight to mid-wicket where Kelly Seymour dropped the catch. My only consolation was that Kelly, our off-spinner, broke a finger in the attempt, so I had to continue bowling!

I did go on to take my only Test wicket, ironically John Gleeson's, whom I yorked. I don't think, though, that I had the

97

same mystifying effect on him! I should have dismissed Connolly as well, but he was dropped off a skier. When Graham Chevalier finally bowled him we went one up in the rubber, winners by 170 runs. The dressing-room rocked in celebration; the three-year exile from the Test arena had left us slightly apprehensive. Now we really had the taste for the big time again.

The scene switched to Kingsmead, where more controversy boiled over before the first ball was bowled. I'm not sure to this day why the two captains tossed up so early, but they did so on the clear understanding that the wicket would receive one more cut before play started. Ali called correctly and decided to bat. Bill Lawry then decided to protest against the extra trimming of the wicket, although in fact it made no difference at all to the outcome; the pitch remained true throughout, and the outfield, parched by a drought, was to be lightning-fast.

Disgruntled from the outset, Australia were on the wrong end of a day in which everything went right for two young South Africans. Graeme Pollock was one; I was the other. Anyone who has ever picked up a bat will understand what I mean when I say it was just one of those days when from the first delivery every ball hit the middle of the bat and with the fast outfield every shot that beat a fielder went for four. Trevor and I began with a partnership of 88, Trevor's share being 17. We went into lunch at 126 for 2, when Ali was bowled round his legs in a kind attempt to give me the strike. I walked in with 94 not out.

Although I realised that a hundred before lunch on the opening session of a Test match would be a rare feat, my prime concern was to make that initial Test ton. I played out a maiden from McKenzie in the penultimate over before the interval. In retrospect if I had known that I would not play again after that series I think I would have chased those extra six runs. It would have put me in the record books in exclusive company; only Trumper, Bradman and Charlie Macartney had done it before.

As it was I had to wait until shortly after lunch to reach three figures. Bill Lawry walked across and shook my hand in congratulation. Despite their habit of abusing you, I have always found Australians more than generous if you have played well. I felt totally elated, and Graeme, who had come in with me after lunch, responded to the atmosphere.

98

I'm sure my innings spurred him to greater heights. After all, he was the young giant of South African cricket. I'd laid down a challenge to him, and although he'd never really been known for enormous scores he played a really unbelievable knock. Together we added a hundred in an hour before my adrenalin ran away with me. I should have set myself for 200, but I tried to whack every ball.

Eventually I missed a slog at Eric Freeman and was bowled for 140. It had taken just three hours and the last 50 came in even time, which in the tempo of Test matches means you are playing a shot to every ball. Along with my triple century and that 70 against Yorkshire in my second county match, I would rate this my best innings of all time. Undoubtedly the best stroke I played came off Gleeson. We had not discovered how to cope with him. Since we could not read the spin the new theory was to take him on and to go down the wicket to him; if you got to the pitch give him a whack, but if you got into trouble, simply use bat and pad to stop the ball getting past. I ran down the wicket and struck him straight for six.

My departure left the stage clear for Graeme. We finished the day at 368 for 5, Pollock 160 not out. Once he was set there was no way they could bowl to him. He had a wide stance, and he simply rocked forward or back and smashed the ball to the boundary. Wherever or whatever they bowled, he hit it for four— 26 boundaries in that 160, an incredibly high proportion. He gave just one chance, behind the wicket off the unlucky Gleeson, when he had scored 104.

Graeme had still not satisfied himself; he batted another three hours on the second day to reach 274, the highest total by a South African in Test cricket, establishing a record 6th-wicket partnership of 200 with Tiger Lance. Ali finally declared at 622 for 9, another record, the largest Test total by South Africa: an unassailable position with the Australians already demoralised because a number of dropped catches—they fielded badly throughout the tour—had prolonged our innings.

We took the field with a real sense of urgency. Our normal competitiveness to win had been sharpened by the petty bickering; we wanted to annihilate Australia. With that enormous total to bowl at, Prockie and Peter Pollock opened at a fearful pace. Keith

Stackpole, who always loved that sort of challenge, responded with a succession of marvellous hooks and cuts. He and Lawry scored 44 at a run a minute, helped of course by the most aggressive of field placings.

They might have survived but for a characteristic intrusion from the man with the golden touch. Eddie Barlow's contribution to our 622 had been 1; he snatched the ball from his captain in his desire to bowl, and in 10 deliveries Australia lost 4 wickets. Barlow claimed Lawry, Chappell—for another 0—and Walters; meanwhile Goddard had Stackpole caught behind by Gamsy. Eight runs later I took my first Test catch, at third slip off Prockie, to send back Redpath.

Our catching was faultless. John Traicos, the Rhodesian off-spinner who was a surprise choice to replace the injured Seymour, took four and only Paul Sheahan held us up. He played beautifully for 62, but Australia followed on a massive 465 runs behind. Their first innings had lasted less than 50 overs.

Stackpole again carried the fight to us and he, Walters and Redpath all reached the 70s, but the first two threw it away when longer application might have saved them. Redpath offered an admirable example in resolution and again took out his bat. He might have frustrated us further but Barlow came back for another spell, his figures at that time 0 for 50, and whittled out Freeman, Taber and McKenzie in quick time. Gleeson stuck with Redpath for an hour and three-quarters, but we finally prised him out to take a 2–0 lead in the series, this time by the margin of an innings and 129 runs.

For the third Test at the Wanderers, Australia left out McKenzie who had been their attacking spearhead for so many years; he, even more than some of his colleagues, had seemed tired and dispirited, not helped by illness. In the two Tests he had not a solitary wicket to his name. The change failed to alter what for the Australians was becoming a dreadfully depressing pattern of events.

Lawry lost the toss again, and though the pitch was green we made 279. But they dropped catches left, right and centre, literally allowing a great opportunity of getting back into the series to slip through their fingers. As early as the second over Goddard was put down at leg-slip, and we put on 56 for the first wicket. At this stage I was playing shots from the first ball. I hooked Lawrie Mayne, McKenzie's replacement, for six, and when I edged Connolly to the wicket-keeper I had raced to 65 off 74 balls with 54 runs in boundaries.

We might have been in deep trouble if Graeme Pollock had not been dropped off simple chances at leg-slip and mid-off; he made 52 and then Lee Irvine, who had played rather tentatively in the previous Tests, found the confidence to play naturally; despite his 79 we were far from happy with our final total. But once more Australia began in suicidal fashion. Lawry skied an attempted hook to Denis Lindsay, who had returned for Gamsy behind the wicket; Stackpole edged a more orthodox catch; and to our extra delight Redpath was lbw to Prockie for 0. Australia were 12 for 3, but they resisted total capitulation. Ian Chappell grafted for more than three hours to make 34, Walters took less time over 64 until he succumbed to his weakness outside the off stump and angled a catch to third slip; Sheahan's easy style brought him 44. But they did have an overlong tail, and 190 for 6 slumped to 202 all out.

I opened our second innings with Eddie Barlow, who justified his promotion by playing the innings of the match. In complete contrast to my performance at Kingsmead I could hardly get the bat to the ball at all, but I suppose the fact that I hung around to make a subdued 35 just reinforced our psychological advantage. Graeme Pollock had no such inhibitions, driving, cutting and pulling his way to an assured 87. The longer our innings continued, the more Australian heads began to droop, especially while Eddie remained at the crease. They had never forgiven him for that incident at Newlands, but he relished the abrasive contest, batting for five hours for 110. Irvine again reached the 70s, and unlike our opponents we batted all the way down the order with Prockie No. 9 on the scorecard. Australia's final target was 486 in 490 minutes. They finished the fourth day at 88 for 5.

Three of those wickets fell to Prockie, and almost inevitably Barlow picked up the other two, Lawry and Ian Chappell, in a typically incisive couple of overs. Only Redpath survived to trouble us on the final day. He found staunch support from Eric Freeman, who was injured, until one of those incidents that always afflicts a demoralised team. Sheahan, who was running for Freeman, ran him out. Within ten minutes 122 for 5 became 126 for 9, with Redpath finally out himself before Connolly and Taber slogged a quick 50.

I finally caught Connolly off Trevor Goddard to bring us victory by a massive 307 runs; only later would we discover that Trevor had taken a wicket with his last ball in Test cricket. The wording of his announcement suggested that he had made an independent decision to retire, but that was not the truth of the matter. Amid the emotional scenes in the dressing-room celebrating our winning of the series, Trevor was huddled in the corner with the selection committee. They were telling him that he would not be picked again, but offering him the opportunity to retire gracefully. As befitting one of the real gentlemen of cricket he did as he was asked, but I thought he was treated very badly. After all he had been the greatest all-rounder South Africa had ever produced. Now it was just a handshake, thanks very much and goodbye.

I was appalled at the ease with which those administrators discarded Trevor. I think Natal gave him a dinner or a cocktail party and made a presentation, but that was all after seventeen years of wonderful service. And they thought they were doing him a big favour. It was the same with Peter Pollock after his tremendously loyal service to Eastern Province; their officials smugly approached him with the news that the board had seen fit to give him a formal dinner. Peter explained in concise detail exactly what they could do with their offer.

There had been no suggestion of a benefit or any financial appreciation until Graeme Pollock became the first beneficiary in 1976. I could see in the treatment of Trevor that however well my career developed, I would one day be on the wrong end of the handshake and all would be forgotten. Our cricket authorities have never appreciated that a professional batsman puts on his pads to make a living. As I say, since I made my point of view very clear, I have always been regarded with suspicion and been stuck with that label of mercenary.

Trevor left one final memory when in his last first-class match he did the hat-trick against Rhodesia at Salisbury. I'm sure he'll forgive me for suggesting that the gods had decreed it. Duncan Fletcher, his first victim, was adjudged caught at the wicket when in fact the ball hit his boot; I caught Errol Laughlin at slip, though to this day Errol swears that the ball came off the pad; and Jackie du Preez was lbw, although he had lunged a long way forward and was struck on the front pad. The joke in the dressing-room was that the umpire was the first person to congratulate Trevor! In the same match I passed Colin Bland's record total for a South African season, finishing with 1,174 runs.

Pat Trimborn was Goddard's replacement for the fourth and final Test at Port Elizabeth. I don't suppose the Aussies could believe it when they lost the toss and had to field yet again. McKenzie had been recalled, but Eddie and I managed the only century opening partnership of the series. Again we exposed their deficiencies in the field; I was dropped off such a simple chance on the leg side that I had begun to walk, and was within a whisker of being run out. Even then I had a funny attitude about the catch being missed. I reckoned the bowler had done well and that I should give him the opportunity to claim my wicket by playing a few shots. I was still a club player at heart; grinding out the runs and making the opposition pay for their mistakes only came as the influence of county cricket grew on me.

I slogged 81; Eddie made 73; but some magnificent bowling from Alan Connolly on the second morning kept us in check. His head never dropped throughout the tour, and his 6 for 47 off 28·2 testing overs held us to 311 all out. But for at least three spilt catches off Gleeson it would have been lower. Again, however, no one could respond with a major innings for Australia. Only Redpath and Sheahan had the stomach to cope with the pace of Peter Pollock and Procter. Trimmie earned his selection by shooting out Ian Chappell and Walters. Two hundred and twelve was their highest first-innings total in the four matches. The captain's call for quick runs was music to my ears.

Keith Miller, in the Melbourne *Sunday News*, wrote kindly of the end product: 'True he was dropped thrice, but look at his style. He took two little skips down the pitch to sweep Gleeson effortlessly over square-leg to bring up his fifty, then he took to Walters, hitting a sizzling hook for four, then lifting him into the packed stand for six. Next in line for the slaughter was McKenzie when Richards stood up straight and banged the ball screaming to the mid-off boundary. Then came the golden stroke of his innings. The next ball from McKenzie was just a fraction short but

Richards with amazing reflexes was across and hit him into the identical spot where he had slammed Walters. This was the stroke of a truly great batsman. He even hit Connolly with an overhead tennis smash to rocket the ball against the mid-on fence. Sure he needs luck. I can say it is great luck for me and the big crowds here to see this new cricketing find in such brilliant mood.'

I finished with 126, but it should have been 111 because Ian Chappell dropped the easiest catch I have ever seen put down in Test cricket, a simple looper to mid-wicket. That life enabled me to pass 500 runs for the series. More catches hit the deck as our innings continued. Lee Irvine took full advantage, actually reaching his maiden Test hundred when Redpath dropped him off a swirling hook down at fine-leg and the ball rolled to the fence. At the declaration Australia were now set 569 to win.

Immediately Peter Pollock pulled a muscle, but it was of no consequence. Though every Australian batsman got set, their highest score was Sheahan's 46. Prockie responded to the extra responsibility by taking 6 for 73, and close to the wicket we caught absolutely everything. We had swept the series, winning each match by progressively larger margins.

Statistics only emphasised our superiority. We had scored six centuries and had achieved five century partnerships to their none; we had averaged 40 runs per wicket throughout the series to their 22. In individual terms nothing could reflect their failure more patently than Ian Chappell's total of 92 runs in 8 innings and Graham McKenzie's series figures of 1 for 333—and that when Ali Bacher trod on his wicket in the last innings of the rubber!

I felt both stimulated and exhausted at the end of the series. Such a flamboyant victory only sweetened the taste for the Test arena, and no sooner had victory been achieved than we were being kitted out with blazers and sweaters for the 1970 tour to England. At the same time the pressure of four years of continuous cricket suddenly hit me, and I began to wonder how long I could continue this yearly round of first-class play. If I was tired at twenty-four, what did the future hold?

Luckily one of the few perks that followed our slaughter of Australia was a free holiday. I took mine in Bangkok and Japan, where I paid a visit to Expo 70, even though I arrived late back for Hampshire's season and missed the first two three-day games. I figured that they would benefit from a refreshed Richards.

South Africa's tour to England was scheduled to start on June 1st. Nine days before that it was cancelled, and I would never play Test cricket again.

Chapter 9

Australian Consolation

I had been one of fourteen players chosen in mid-March 1970 to represent South Africa in England. For the record the other thirteen were A. Bacher (Captain), E. J. Barlow (Vice-Captain), R. G. Pollock, B. L. Irvine, D. Lindsay, H. R. Lance, M. J. Procter, P. M. Pollock, P. H. J. Trimborn, A. J. Traicos, A. M. Short, G. L. G. Watson and G. A. Chevalier. Apart from Prockie and me, who were contracted to play for our counties, the party got no further than net practices in Durban, which must have been conducted in an atmosphere similar to wartime exercises in preparation for a mission that was continually aborted.

The analogy with war is far from irrelevant. Until I returned to England my appreciation, as usual, of the hardening of public opinion had been less than perceptive. The 'Stop the Seventy Tour' committee, led by Peter Hain, had set such a precedent with disruptive demonstrations at rugby matches that Lord's, that very haven of sportsmanship, was surrounded by undignified barbed wire. Though cricket-lovers established the '1970 Cricket Fund', with its aim of financing precautions against anti-South African protests, the 'Fair Cricket Campaign', another anti-tour body, added its weight to the dispute. Already the first month of the original full tour had been axed.

On 18th May, the Cricket Council pledged their support to the tour—a statement which only encouraged the demonstrators to outline more massive threats to social order. Our players were regularly criticised for failing to speak out against apartheid, a silence which was misinterpreted as acceptance of the policy. I have explained my own political views in the first chapter of this book; at the time I could only agree with Ali Bacher, who said that he totally accepted the right to protest, providing that no violence ensued and that play was not interrupted.

None of the demonstrating bodies would give such an indication. Naturally the question had now reached government level. The Cricket Council had little alternative but to grant the Home Secretary's request to call off the tour. Having spent three weeks in England, testing the temperature, I was far from surprised; but strange as it may seem today, I *still* felt that it was only a temporary reverse.

For the two Pollocks, Barlow, Prockie and myself came the consolation prize of places in the Rest of the World squad, hastily assembled for five unofficial 'tests' against England. Actually the contests never had the authentic atmosphere of a country versus country conflict; the heady emotions of our win against Australia remained firmly imprinted in my heart. On our side there was a very free-and-easy approach; no one minded if you arrived at a ground a quarter of an hour late. England may have taken it more seriously, especially as the prize money was considerable. We felt so blessed with talent within our side that we were always going to win.

An innings victory in the opener at Lord's only reinforced that belief, but then we caught a cold at Trent Bridge. I spent the series making 30s and 40s but I managed 64 at Nottingham before that golden touch of Tony Greig somehow induced me to play a leg-glance into Alan Knott's gloves. Ray Illingworth, who had a magnificent series with the bat, kept his side on an even keel with 97 in the first innings and then, after our wickets had been rather hastily tossed away for the second time in the match, Brian Luckhurst ground England to an 8-wicket victory with a patient 113 not out.

Suitably rapped over the knuckles, we then won the other three games, though England might have levelled the series at Headingley. We needed a mere 223 to win, a snip for such a glittering line-up, but at the end of the fourth day the scoreboard read 75 for 5. Worse still, Kanhai had an injured finger; and I had damaged my back diving to catch D'Oliveira and had not batted in the first innings.

For a long time the next morning it seemed the crisis had

passed. Sobers and Intikhab, who had escaped a chance when for once Greig's hands lost some of their magic, gradually pushed towards victory. But at 177 Snow had Garfield caught at slip, which sent in Prockie; apart from Lance Gibbs he was our last fit man. Inti immediately holed out on the boundary, and Rohan, marginally more mobile than I, edged Illingworth to the wicket-keeper.

I had been off the field since the first day of the match but I gingerly went to the wicket; the score was 183 for 8. At 201 Snow took the new ball, and the whole England side leapt in the air when one delivery flew off my pad into Don Wilson's hands at short-leg. Don remains convinced that I edged it on to my leg, but I can assure him that I never touched the ball with my bat. At the time all the fielders were very tense because the winning team would receive £2,000.

Shortly after that I went down the wicket and told Prockie to take it very gently; we had plenty of time. He nodded and then wound into a big drive over mid-off for four off the very next ball. A few balls later he sliced another slog through the slips for a second boundary. I don't know what he would have done if I had told him to get after the bowling! Between us we gathered the winning runs.

I was very aware that the cosmopolitan composition of our side kept all the South Africans in the political limelight. For those who looked for the first sign of dressing-room discord, I can assure you that there was none. Black or white, we had total respect for each other as cricketers, and enjoyed each other's company. Though the series fell a long way short of what had been cancelled, it was a rewarding and enjoyable experience.

It helped break up the repetition of the county circuit, which I had already begun to find wearing. Some players were dissatisfied with Roy Marshall's captaincy to the extent that their concern was reported back to the committee. I refused to get involved; if there was to be a change I would happily play under a new captain.

I had learnt a lot from Roy Marshall. On the field he exhibited tremendous knowledge about the game, but he was never a great communicator or motivator. If he had a major fault, it was that he used to judge every player by his own extremely high standards; he could not easily accept the shortcomings of others. He was not the type who roused his team in a dynamic way, but at reading situations out there in the middle he was always impressive. I would not find out until I returned the following season that Richard Gilliat had been appointed to take his place.

Though I missed several championship matches I topped the county averages, my highest score, 153, including a hundred before lunch against Derbyshire at Chesterfield. But there was more controversy: I got a fine edge to the very first delivery of the match, from Alan Ward, and Bob Taylor held up the catch. I did not walk because I was sure it hadn't carried. Bob said it was a fair catch, which is usually accepted by the batsman. I was still not sure and the umpire at square leg gave me not out. There was not much applause from the Derbyshire players when I reached the hundred.

Though I had come to terms with the batting problems on English wickets, I was conscious that South Africa were to tour Australia in 1971–72. Gaining some experience of their conditions was one of the reasons I accepted an offer from the Prospect Club in Adelaide for the preceding season. An opportunity to earn the sort of money I could not at that time make in South Africa provided another justification. The sheer excitement of travel appealed to me as well.

I was criticised at home for turning my back on the Currie Cup, but had Natal made a counter-offer I would have stayed. I told them that I had received an attractive proposal, but I got no response. No one leapt and said 'Don't go', or 'Wouldn't you like us to employ you so that you can play Currie Cup cricket?' So I went, and I fell in love with Australia.

The entire deal was splendidly organised. Coca-Cola provided me with a car and a salary; the Prospect Club took care of my accommodation. And, as became very well known, the manufacturers of 'The Real Thing' sponsored me for a dollar a run. What was less publicised was that I was also on 10 dollars a wicket, but that was probably because I had little opportunity to bowl. At a welcoming get-together Terry Jenner, the Australian leg-spinner, introduced himself to me and practically the first words he said were: 'I hear you're an off-spinner, but you're not going to bowl for our club because Rowdy (Ashley Mallett) bowls one end and I bowl the other.' Some welcome!

In fact the club gladly accepted me, and we had a very strong side: Jeff Hammond, the opening bowler who toured England in 1972, brought our complement to four present or future Test players. The club also offered a wide variety of social activities, much more so than in South Africa. I still write regularly to Reg Craig, who was the coach, and who really went out of his way to make me feel at home.

Apart from playing, I was engaged to coach and undertake promotional work for my sponsors, along with two other sports-men, Greg Chappell and Kerry O'Brien—the steeplechaser who tragically crashed into one of the hurdles when he looked set to win the gold medal at the Munich Olympic Games. Kitted out in special uniforms, we did the circuit of lunch and dinner speaking engagements.

But the biggest perk of all was being chosen to represent South Australia for the season. There had been no guarantee when I signed with Prospect; simply that they would put my name for-ward for selection. They took a chance on me at the start, because within Australian cricket certain objections had been raised against playing foreigners. I like to think that I returned the favour.

But this was only after a repeat performance of my county championship début. My first innings for South Australia came in a one-day competition against Victoria. Again I batted at No. 4—Ashley Woodcock and John Causby were the recognised opening pair—and I was caught at the wicket for 0. I can remember Bill Lawry dancing a jig of delight at mid-off, and a few caustic com-ments from the crowd along similar lines to those of the Sussex fielders in 1968.

In the first Sheffield game against Western Australia at Adelaide I did open; Causby scored 115 batting at No. 6. In the first innings a ball from Graham McKenzie bounced a little and I was caught at leg-slip for 7, but in the second innings, in pursuit of a ridiculous declaration, I finished 44 not out. Even though Terry Jenner and Ashley Mallett were both playing, Ian Chappell gave me a bowl in their second innings and I took 3 for 29, including Rod Marsh caught at slip. It must have been a turning wicket!

Four days later we provided the opposition for the MCC's opening first-class match of the tour. My single memory of the first day is of Geoff Boycott. I arrived at the ground before the start of play and Geoff had already been in the nets for half an hour. He then batted all day for 173 not out before going back for another session of practice after stumps. The second day began the same way: another long net. But in the first or second over he gently guided an easy-paced delivery down the leg side into the keeper's gloves: 173 out. Somehow it seemed hilarious, such a tame departure after all that preparation.

I was conscious of a beautiful opportunity to make runs in a match of some prestige which would be reported worldwide. Contrary to accusations that the payment per run altered my attitude—remarks which were to annoy me all season, because in all honesty the incentive made no conscious difference—I just set about batting responsibly and professionally.

When I was bowled by Basil D'Oliveira, a ball which kept low, I had made 224 in six and a quarter hours; this time I did not slog until I had passed 200. Everyone made runs as we finally declared at 649 for 9; most of mine were scored in long partnerships with Ian and Greg Chappell. The tourists did not have a very athletic fielding side and we took a run for virtually every ball. With Gary Player winning the Dunlop International in Canberra at the same time, it was a great day for South Africa.

On such a good wicket, the MCC had no difficulty playing out for a draw with D'Oliveira making a hundred, a feat he was to repeat in the second match between the tourists and South Australia. I moved on to play against Victoria on a Melbourne wicket, which was a little damper than the normal fast, true pitches in Australia which are such a joy to batsmen.

My initial impression of the Melbourne Cricket Ground was its sheer vastness; in fact I was dropped at fine-leg off a hook which on most grounds in the world would have been a comfortable six. As usual I managed to put some extra pressure on myself because Victoria fielded Alan 'Froggy' Thomson (no relation to Jeff) in their attack. He was their bright new hope, and was to play in four Tests that series and collect a bundle of Shield wickets. Naturally I told reporters prior to the match that I would be facing him with confidence; the printed version of my comments suggested that I had said I would smash him all over the place. Actually I was one of his seven victims in the first innings, but not before I had made 52.

We then flew to Perth. On the day before the start of our return match with Western Australia I took my usual net practice, at the end of which I felt quite apprehensive. Every time a bowler slipped himself the ball flew off the track like lightning; moreover the pre-game ballyhoo had centred around a young, fiery fast bowler who was on the verge of playing for Australia. Dennis Lillee had missed the match in Adelaide; now he and Graham McKenzie would share the new ball, a formidable partnership on what was then a wicket as quick as any in the world.

Ian Chappell won the toss, and I opened with John Causby. I am indebted to Rodney Marsh for his version of that day, Friday 21st November 1970. McKenzie ran in, in that wonderfully co-ordinated style, and bowled the first ball of the match, a gentle outswinger which I felt for and missed. As Rod tossed the ball back round the field he turned to John Inverarity, the first slip, and said: 'Geez, I thought this bloke was supposed to be able to play a bit.' That evening when Lillee bowled the last ball of the day, I simply walked down the wicket, drove the ball back past him to the sight screen for four and without breaking stride continued towards the pavilion: 325 not out. Inverarity turned to Marsh, with remarkably quick recall considering the hours in the field, and commented cryptically: 'I suppose he can play a bit.'

Rod always jokes that he gave a faultless performance behind the stumps because that first delivery was the only one to pass the bat; in fact as our batsman demolished their attack he brilliantly stumped Ian Chappell for 129 after we had put on 308 in 170 minutes, and then threw himself to catch Greg Chappell off McKenzie. Well though Western Australia fielded, we ended the five and a half hours of that opening day at 513 for 3.

Recalling that innings now is like a dream. Somehow I managed to sustain for a complete day the sort of form that usually material-ises only in short, glorious moments. Conditions, of course, could have been no better, and I think the quality of their attack, which also included Tony Lock, helped me to maintain a higher than usual level of concentration. It all began with a quarter of an hour of reconnaissance before I got off the mark, a period of adjustment to the pace of that delightful wicket.

My first runs came from a square drive off the back foot which I hardly struck, but the ball flew past point for four. So fast did the ball come on to the bat that every nudge sped to the boundary. By lunch I had made 79 in a fairly steady way, but in the next session Ian and I sailed into their spinners. We matched each other shot for shot and I progressed from 100 to 200 in only 84 minutes. Lockie became more and more frustrated, particularly when he fielded at mid-off to the leg-spin of Ian Brayshaw. I drove one ball for four which Tony dived at and just missed. He dropped ten yards deeper for the next; but the only result was another despairing dive and another four. He backed off further still, but I still managed to place my shot just outside his reach as he flung himself to the ground again.

Brayshaw should have had me out at 169. I lofted an on-drive off McKenzie straight to him at mid-on but he missed the chance. He told me later that at the time he didn't expect it to be an expensive miss, because it looked from my slogging as though I would throw my wicket away at any moment. In fact it cost him 187 runs. The only other chance I gave was from the shot which brought my 300, on the third man boundary of all places. Mind you, only a fielder as athletic as Bob Meuleman, who was a champion squash player, would have got a hand to what was really a mis-cue as I tried a cross-batted shot over cover.

As you might expect, I was also on the receiving end of a few curses from Lillee, particularly when I had my moments of fortune against him with a couple of unconvincing hooks which dropped safely and dribbled to the boundary. But for the rest it was a performance which will warm my twilight years. One of my real regrets in life is that although two television stations covered the day's play, neither has any recording. ABC searched high and low for it, but with no success. The only souvenir I have is a three-minute film taken by a friend of mine, which is not very clear but does include a shot of the scoreboard at the end of play.

After being rushed off for various interviews I spent a surprisingly quiet evening with my team-mates; the sense of elation kept away the tiredness, but painting the town was not really my style. And I still had to continue the innings the next day, though I was to last only another 42 minutes.

It took a terrible lbw decision to get me out. Tony Mann, who was to become a team-mate in the same grade side in Perth six years later, had set a far-flung field with the only noticeable gap at fine-leg. When he bowled a full toss which was going down the leg side, I tried to paddle the ball into that open space, not an easy shot. I missed and 'Rocket' Mann, a purveyor of almighty appeals in true Australian fashion, gave full vent in his most pleading manner. Warren Carter gave me out; 'Rocket' and I still maintain he was sick and tired of seeing me at the crease.

I finished with 356, having batted for 372 minutes—and for those of you who like a statistical record, I scored 100 in 125 minutes, 200 in 209 minutes and 300 in 317 minutes; in all I hit one six and 48 fours. The figures that perhaps I savour the most, and I apologise to my good friend for reminding him, belonged to Dennis Lillee—18 overs, 1 maiden, 117 runs, no wickets. We then bowled Western Australia out twice for our first victory of the season, a result which set us on course to become the champions.

The saga of Perth had not yet finished. I had persuaded Lorna, a lovely girl who had become very important to me, to fly out to Australia. Because Perth is an international airport, but Adelaide is not, we had planned her arrival to coincide with the last day of the Western Australia match. Her flight was due around half past four or five o'clock the following morning. The day after we had won the game Greg and Ian Chappell and I celebrated our victory with suitable fervour and, when Greg left around two in the morning, I decided that it would be pointless trying to sleep. Ian let me down by nodding off in mid-conversation. Still holding a glass of lager I dozed off as well, and the next thing I knew it was six o'clock and the beer had spilled all over me. I raced to the airport praying that the flight had been delayed, but of course it had been right on schedule. Poor Lorna, not knowing a soul in the country apart from me, was in a terrible state. Her first words were punctuated with comments which made Dennis Lillee's curses seem rather tame. There were further traumas when we finally arrived back in Adelaide, where my flat had been burgled by a thief who obviously read the cricket reports.

It was almost a month before the next first-class game, South Australia's second match against the MCC. This time I retained some of the shots but not all of the patience. Ashley Woodcock and I began with a partnership of 250 on a day that was interrupted by rain. After 280 minutes of concentration I just tossed my wicket away in the last over of the day, stumped by Bob Taylor off Derek Underwood for 146. It was Underwood as a batsman, hanging around for two hours with D'Oliveira, who saved his side in the fourth innings.

I began to be perturbed when critics described my 35 against Queensland as a 'failure'; after all, not too many players average that score throughout a career. But Greg Chappell and Ken Cunningham rapped centuries, and we chalked up another victory by an innings and plenty. I might have really failed in the return match at Brisbane because Tony Dell, the Queensland left-arm opening bowler who was to play for Australia that season, had me groping with the extra bounce he achieved from his big frame. I really struggled to reach double figures, but then smoothed out some of the kinks to finish with another century, this time 155; unfortunately we could not prise out John Maclean to earn the precious extra points for an outright win.

Against New South Wales in Sydney I again profited from a missed catch; this time by John Benaud at slip off Dave Renneberg when I had made only 6; John took the next chance I offered him, but by then I had moved on to 178. It was a challenging experience, that day, working out a technique to combat a new young spinner, David Hourn, who would develop later into a regular wicket-taker in Shield cricket. But because of rain our title hopes took another knock, and we finished without a point from that game.

There are times when whatever you do you feel that you are going to make runs, and my hot streak continued into our next match, against Victoria at the Adelaide Oval. My scores were 105 and 72, but Alan Sieler dismissed me both times with his little left-arm seamers at around medium pace. Sieler was still appearing for Victoria in 1977, and, as he was also a more than useful batsman, I was always waiting for him to develop into a top-class performer. But, as with Trevor Jesty of Hampshire, it has been a case of threatening but not consistently producing. Kerry Mackay of Queensland was another who impressed me during that season, but he also came into that category of player.

A massive 221 from Ken Eastwood took Victoria to a first-innings victory in another drawn match. Eastwood, who was thirty-five, could not even command a place in their side at the start of the season, but he was to score 737 runs in only six

WESTERN AUSTRALIA CRICKET CLUB V SOUTH AUSTRALIA C. CLUB

HOME CLUB   VISITORS

FIRST INNINGS OF SOUTH AUSTRALIA   PLAYED AT W.A.C.A.   ON 20,21, Nov 19 70

#	BATSMEN	TIME IN	OUT	RUNS SCORED	SCORING RATE 50	100	150	HOW OUT	BOWLER	TOTAL
1	B.A. RICHARDS	11	12	144|43|24|11|34|23|24|22|4|3|12|111|43||24|4|11|244|11|44|||4|4|4|23|	70	125	176	LBW	MANN	356
				2|14|12|||124|4|2|4||23|1|44|62|44|111|2|11|3||111||22||14|11||2|111|42|111|22|41|(cont)	200	150	200			
2	J. CAUSBY	11 30	12 59	113|42||111|42|311|42|14||4|11 (RICHARDS)	209	346	317	c CHADWICK	LOCK	58
				(cont) 2|2|4|111|42|2|4|44|111|4+11						
				(cont) 44|22|2|4|12|4|14+11		350				
							304			
3	I. CHAPPELL	1	51	14+1|4|11|32|111|44|12|111|2|14+4|21|44|2|14|4|214|2|111|2|3|11|4|111|2|2|2|2|2|2|	83	139		st MARSH	LOCK	129
				4|4+11|4|41|61						
4	G. CHAPPELL	4 53	5 48	12|2|4|2				c MARSH	McKENZIE	11
5	K. CUNNINGHAM	5 20	12 15	11|11|111|111				c INVERARITY	LOCK	13
6	J. LANGLEY	12 14	12 57	2|41				RUN OUT		7
7	E. FREEMAN	12 18	12 05	14|1				c IRVINE	LOCK	6
8	R. BLUNDELL	12 27	12 30	1|1|1|1				BOWLED	MANN	0
9	A. MALLETT	12 32	12 47					NOT OUT		6
10	T. JENNER	12 37	12 47	13|1				c McKENZIE	MANN	5
11	J. HAMMOND							DID NOT BAT		-

RICHARDS 18 x FOURS: 1 x 6:   I. CHAPPELL 13 x FOURS; 1 x 6: FOURS: 2 x 6:

INNINGS 407 MINS:

RESULT

INNINGS / TIMES:
50 - 47m
100 - 83m
150 - 116m
200 - 151m
250 - 160m
300 - 205m
350 - 233m
400 - 286m
450 - 297m
500 - 322m
550 - 368m

	RUNS AT THE FALL OF EACH WICKET AND NO. OF OUTGOING BATSMAN									
	1	2	3	4	5	6	7	8	9	10
1	109	417	447	551	553	563	563	564	575	
2	3	4		5	5	7	8	6	10	

BOWLERS	OVERS	MDN'S	RUNS	WKTS	AVGE	BALLS B'WLD	NO BALLS	WIDES
1 G. McKENZIE	19	2	101	4	-	152	3	
2 D. LILLEE	18	1	117	-	-	144	1	
3 J. BRAMSHAW	12	1	69	-	-	96	2	
4 A. MANN	20.6	1	120	3	-	166		
5 A. LOCK	16	1	108	4	-	128		
6 J. INVERARITY	8	-	56	-	-	64		
7								
8			EXT 4					
	93.6	6	575	9	-	750		

EXTRAS 4

TOTAL 575 FOR 9 (dec) WKTS.

BYES

LEG BYES

WIDES

NO BALLS IIII

UMPIRES 1 ..... N. TOWNSEND .....   2 ..... W. CARTER .....   SCORERS 1 .....   2 .....

GAME STARTED .... GAME FINISHED .....

Fig. 2. My record-breaking innings for South Australia in November 1970. Dennis Lillee took 0 for 117

completed innings. He even replaced Bill Lawry for the final Test but failed in both knocks in the match in which England regained the Ashes.

A marvellous bowling performance from Eric Freeman against New South Wales—13 for 115 in the match—in the end brought us the Sheffield Shield, though for me it was a painful finale. In my first innings a ball from David Colley jumped off a length and rapped against my bottom hand; it stung so much that I had a huge slog at the next delivery, but though the ball whistled over long leg for six, the ache did not ease. I had hit that six with a broken finger.

I would not have batted the second time around, but with wickets falling, a few quick runs were required to establish a platform for Ian's declaration. I went in at No. 8 or 9 after Geoff Davies had taken 5 wickets with his leg-spinners, and using only the top hand I somehow pieced together a few boundaries. Quite rightly Renneberg then returned to the attack and his very first ball struck glove, splint, finger and all. I took the discreet course and retired hurt.

We might have landed the double by winning the V & G knockout competition, but for the only piece of bad captaincy I ever saw from Ian Chappell. In the semi-finals against Queensland, who did not win a match in the Shield, our 261 for 6 should certainly have been a winning score. But instead of just containing, Ian opted to bowl them out to win, a strategy which included using Ashley Mallett from the end which had a short leg-side boundary. Tom Graveney, in his stint as the Queensland coach, could hardly believe his eyes. Rowdy bowled and Tom swept and lapped him for six: again and again. We finally got him out for 98, but the damage had been done. Ian had never conceived that they could pass our total, but they did with overs to spare.

That apart, my only disappointment was with the structure of grade cricket: one match being played over two successive Saturdays, so that I only managed ten innings for the Prospect Club, whose invitation had brought about this wonderful season. In first-class matches, I could hardly have been more pleased with my final total of 1,538 runs at an average of 109·86. I fell short of Don Bradman's record of 1,690 runs for New South Wales in

1928–29, but it was an honour to come that close to the great man whose company I so enjoyed several times during that season.

'The Don' kindly spoke at a celebration dinner organised by Coca-Cola at the end of the year, one of a number of tributes which touched me enormously, gestures which I am sure no other country would have taken the trouble to make. I was much honoured by the award of the Viscount Hampden Trophy as South Australia's most valuable cricketer; Coca-Cola presented me with a beautiful salver and six silver goblets, five of the goblets representing the five states against each of which I had scored a century and the sixth representing the MCC. Each is inscribed with the dates of those hundreds and the actual scores. The inscription on the salver read: 'In appreciation from Coca-Cola for what you did for South Australia'. Even Western Australia, on the wrong end of that triple century, made a presentation of a water jug and a matching tray engraved 'To Barry Richards—325 in a day—a super knock'. Wonderful treasures that my mother guards for me at home in Durban until I finally put down roots in one place.

Each gift was totally unexpected because, after all, I was being paid a generous salary. But perhaps the most amazing tribute of all came from that great old leg-spinner Bill O'Reilly, writing in the Sydney *Morning Herald*. He flatteringly suggested that Australia and England should toss a coin for the use of my services in the Test series. It would be utterly churlish, however, not to point out that I had been able to play the best cricket of my life in the context of a wonderfully enthusiastic and talented team, all of whom should take credit for my personal triumphs.

I left Australia hoping in my own mind that I would be returning the following season as a member of the South African touring party. En route for England I stopped off in South Africa for one final match of the season, a trial for the tour. I guested for Transvaal against the Rest of South Africa. Arriving after a long flight just thirty-six hours before a festival game, I found myself in an atmosphere that was more funereal than festive.

A month earlier, in March 1971, the South African Cricket Association had attempted to build a bridge over the differences between the Association and the Cricket Council; they informed the government that they wanted to invite the non-white South African Cricket Boards to nominate two non-white players to be considered on merit for inclusion of the Springbok team to go to Australia. On 2nd April, my first full day home, and the day before the start of the match, the government announced its categorical rejection of the proposition. Another bridge had been demolished.

Five or six senior players, including myself, decided that now was the time for the players to speak out, though some of the Transvaal fellows and those who were not established top-level cricketers were worried about the repercussions. But finally everyone agreed on an act of protest. When the game began the following morning I took a single from Prockie's first ball, and then batsmen and fielders left the pitch to gasps of astonishment from the spectators. Before resuming play all twenty-two players presented the Cricket Association officials with the following written statement: 'We cricketers feel that the time has come for an expression of our views. We fully support the South African Cricket Association's application to invite non-whites to tour Australia, if they are good enough, and further subscribe to merit being the only criterion on the cricket field.' Frank Waring, the Minister of Sport, had invited both teams to his house for a barbecue that night. He cancelled it.

Sensationalistic the protest may have been; futile it probably was; but by now we were beginning to feel the real possibility of being cast out from the Test scene. Despite overt welcoming noises from Australia other, less friendly sounds were more in evidence; there were demonstrations during a South African rugby tour of the country. Despite all the adverse signs the SACA picked another touring party; even for the players it was more an act of hope than expectation.

The honour, at least of selection, went to A. Bacher (Captain), E. J. Barlow (who later withdrew for business reasons and was replaced by A. M. Short), P. D. de Vaal, B. L. Irvine, C. E. B. Rice, H. M. Ackerman, G. A. Chevalier, A. L. Biggs, P. M. Pollock, R. G. Pollock, M. J. Procter, D. Lindsay, B. A. Richards, P. H. J. Trimborn and V. A. P. van der Bijl. But on September 8th the barrier was dropped. The severance of connections with Australia now meant complete isolation.

Even the trial match had gone badly from a personal viewpoint. Because of my much publicised incentives in Australia, Prockie and I had been offered 2 rand per run; some of the other twenty players were hardly delighted at this discrimination. Prockie already had his own stimulus, because he came into the game after equalling the world record of C. B. Fry and Bradman of six successive first-class hundreds. But his attempt to break it ended after he had moved smoothly to 22; then he pulled Peter de Vaal for four, but in doing so trod on his wicket.

In my one and only appearance for Transvaal I made 140 and 67. Disappointing? Well, it brought down my average for the season!

Chapter 10

Summers of Discontent

The turn of the political screw against South Africa meant I would play the next seven English seasons uninterrupted with Hampshire. As I write in September 1977, I remain under contract for two further years, though the repercussions of my allegiance to Kerry Packer make the future uncertain.

Though I shall always feel the greatest affection for Hampshire for allowing me to savour county cricket, as I've said earlier I have been disillusioned for a considerable time. Though it has been a voluntary sentence, I have felt like a prisoner within the system.

The routine is interminable: every match is a carbon copy of the last. You travel to away matches, often on journeys that have more in common with a mystery tour than a drive to work. You reach the hotel. You book in. You go downstairs for a few drinks. You go out to a Berni Inn, you feed on steak and chips, you come back and go to bed. You wake up in the morning. You have your breakfast. You read the papers. You have a cup of tea. You go to the ground. You have another cup of tea. You play the day's cricket. You have another drink. And you go back to the hotel and the routine starts again, day after day after day *ad nauseam*.

For many professionals, it is an idyllic life, with countless hours spent playing or talking about cricket. Though for several seasons I loved to be on the field—an attitude that has begun to wane—I could never sustain my interest through the regular post-play debates that fascinated many of my colleagues. I had also been brought up on the importance of fitness and when I first arrived I took a very intolerant view of any regular after-match socialising. During the season, no counties appear to demand any special exercise in the cause of fitness—hampered, I do accept, by the tight cricket schedule—nevertheless a completely different approach from that in South Africa, where the basically amateur attitudes are reflected in a burning enthusiasm to maintain the highest level of preparation.

To be realistic, seven days a week of cricket would dampen, both physically and mentally, the eagerness of most lovers of the game. By 1977 I had become so disenchanted that even a hundred before lunch left me with no sense of elation. Conversely the bitter disappointments after a nought, and the ensuing hours of smouldering self-reproach, are also moods of the past. The ritual has left me totally numb.

The problem was not helped by the expectations levelled at me. If I scored a hundred, I had only achieved what was expected; I hadn't actually surprised anyone. If I got out for anything less, I had failed. Moreover as the seasons passed I was expected to reach three figures in quicker and quicker time. A three-hour hundred was accepted and praised as a fast innings in 1968, but it has now got to be in two hours. Today's three-hour century is usually described as 'a subdued knock'.

You might then wonder why I have stayed in the county game for so long. Money, of course, has been important, though we are back to the mercenary tag. Are you a mercenary if you are trying to safeguard your future? Surely not. Many county cricketers settle for the thrill of participating in the game living out their dreams. When the axe drops at thirty-five they sort out their problems from there. I envy that approach because I have always worried what I would do when I was no longer good enough to earn a living from cricket. Hence the prospect of a benefit, which I was awarded in 1977, offered financial light at the end of a murky tunnel.

But I also stayed because much of the monotony disappeared in a run of success, which brought us victories in the County championship and the John Player League. Changes on the staff, too, not only improved the atmosphere in the dressing-room from my earlier years but also, probably to our own surprise, fashioned a winning side.

The initial alteration came at the top. I returned in 1971 to find that Roy Marshall had been relieved of the captaincy in favour of Richard Gilliat. At the end of the season the county lost two opening bowlers. Butch White, who had struggled to combat knee trouble, was not re-engaged in an unhappy episode, in which the former England player was bitterly disappointed at the county's decision. In the case of Bob Cottam, the most penetrative member of our attack, the decision to leave was entirely voluntary. Only three years after being voted the best young cricketer in England, Bob had become disillusioned with the county. Since the feeling was not mutual Hampshire opposed the transfer of his registration, but by mid-June of 1972 he was permitted to play for Northamptonshire.

With Derek Shackleton now retired and our bowling dangerously weakened, I envisaged most of the season being spent in the field. The replacements, an architect and two rejects from other counties, hardly suggested that bonus points for bowling would become our specialty. Middlesex had flirted with Bob Herman for several seasons before releasing him. Hampshire probably gave him a second chance because he was Southampton-born, and also because he was the son of O. W. 'Lofty' Herman, a former fast bowler for the county and at that time a first-class umpire. 'Lofty junior' could swing the ball prodigiously at a brisk pace if he got his action right. Fortunately for us he sustained his skills magnificently for four seasons until 1976, when his whole rhythm disappeared; and he would have been unable to bowl straight if there had been twelve stumps instead of three. In 1972, however, he could not have had a greater impact, with 75 wickets in the County championship, 30 more than any other of our bowlers.

Making his début that season with a background of nothing more substantial than university cricket was Tom Mottram, who had moved into the area to work as an architect in Poole. Well over 6 ft tall and as thin as a rake, he looked in the nets more of an academic than an opening bowler, and his comic walk, long strides with his arms down by his side, immediately earned him the nickname of 'Pink Panther'. Pretty soon we would be calling him 'Tom Magic' or 'Merlin the Magician' because his great virtues of line and length would bring in hauls of victims. Many county batsmen would joke that when Tom took the new ball, the danger instead of being caught in the slips, was of holing out at mid-off; but the 'Pink Panther' often had the last laugh.

Released by Nottinghamshire after eleven years at Trent Bridge, Mike Taylor became another new signing at the start of the 1973 season. Perhaps having been so long in a relatively unsuccessful side had blunted some of his edge, but he joined us with the keenness of a man with a point or two to prove. In the middle of the previous year Dave O'Sullivan, the New Zealand slow left-armer, had won a place in the side and taken some important wickets.

No more mixed bag had set out since the Canterbury pilgrims but, to our own amazement, we finished the 1973 journey along the highways and byways of the County championship ahead of the pack. Our batting had always been a strength, with Gordon Greenidge making a huge stride forward from a cavalier but care-less cricketer into a world-class opening partner. David Turner—who has been unlucky not to represent his country because several inferior performers with the bat have won caps—and the captain, in his highly individual style, have been prolific scorers. If Trevor Jesty often represented unfulfilled promise at that stage—he did not make a first-class hundred in England until he was twenty-eight—he was a more than handy 'bits and pieces' player, while Peter Sainsbury in his fortieth year produced marvellous figures with bat and ball—including his first century in nine seasons.

Two early wins over Sussex and Yorkshire did not kindle any fires in our ambitions. The memory of Gordon's magnificent 196 at Headingley, where he struck a ball from Tony Nicholson into the houses outside the ground, would sustain us during the long and wearisome days that would inevitably be spent in the field when the weather dried and the wickets improved. But we followed up with successive victories at Swansea and Coventry. I missed the Glamorgan match where Trevor Jesty bowled them out in the first innings for 110 and Sains tricked them for even less in the second, but I had recovered for Warwickshire.

The Coventry ground is not particularly large; the wicket on the first day is usually pretty true. I managed to take advantage of the combination to make my highest score in England, 240 of which 170 came in boundaries. I am always a little chary of

Warwickshire because David Brown has a good record against me in England, probably because he always bowls a full length knowing that I'll go for the shot and that any late movement might defeat me. But not this time.

Our close fielding, which was to back the attack so splendidly throughout the year, was a major factor in enforcing the follow-on; then 'Tom Magic' went to town, whittling his way through a strong batting side to finish with 6 for 63. Though Bob Willis took 3 wickets, including mine, in 4 overs, we chalked up another win by 7 wickets.

By now, the second week of June, we had overtaken Essex at the head of the table, but our next match against Surrey at Portsmouth brought back the old doubts. A partnership of 207 between Gordon, 99, and myself, 116, had overtaken Surrey's first-innings score, and in the end they batted again 163 behind. This time I really felt confident in our attack because the ball was seaming more and more, but Surrey easily survived through the final day to finish in the sanctuary of 281 for 5. Many a championship hope of the previous week was dismissed as self-deception in the dressing-room after that day's play.

But though our next four matches were drawn, with a trouncing from the West Indians sandwiched in the middle, there was no plummeting down the table. Northamptonshire enjoyed a spell at the top, and in doing so took the pressure from us. After all, to the critics and the public we seemed to be in a false position—and, if the truth be told, to ourselves as well. But a flourish at the end of July was to change that.

It began at Southport, where an innings victory over Lancashire lifted us back on top. We were never to be headed again. Richard put them in, but on a slow pitch they batted feebly. A few minutes after tea Gordon and I began our reply, another partnership in which we both struck our best form at the same time. At 200, Farokh Engineer caught me behind the wicket off Jack Simmons for 128; Gordon thrashed on merrily to 153. Jesty and Mottram ensured that Lancashire would fashion no second-innings recovery.

The following day Norman Gifford put us in at Worcester, but for three innings bat dominated ball, particularly on the third morning when we cracked 219 in 110 minutes, Greenidge 104, to enable Richard to declare. Peter Sainsbury, the only survivor from Hampshire's previous championship win in 1961, already had the scent of the end of a twelve-year wait. He bowled out the top of the order while Mike Taylor extinguished the rest, and we won with more than an hour to spare.

August was to belong to 'Daffy' O'Sullivan, a harvest of wickets in what, ironically, turned out to be his last full month with the county. His 6 for 35 on the last day almost brought us an improbable victory in a rain-ruined match against Essex; Fletcher, Pont, Hardie and East all fell caught Richards bowled O'Sullivan. But four successive wins would bring the champagne of victory to a county which began the season with very much a 'light ale' tag.

Dour Derbyshire were the first victims, by 10 wickets. In the match they made 379 runs; it took them 234·5 overs, but O'Sullivan with 4 wickets in the first innings and Sainsbury with 5 in the second outlasted even their patience. Gilliat's rapid hundred could have been in no starker contrast. But a far more important triumph followed.

Northamptonshire came to Southampton in second place. Jim Watts, their captain, will always wonder whether a gamble in that match might have changed the destination of the title. I'm certain he thought long and hard after winning the toss, but he followed the old dictum and still decided to bat. On a day where Herman, Mottram, Jesty and Taylor in their differing styles made the ball swing and seam, Northamptonshire sat down to lunch at 60-odd for 8.

They struggled to 108 all out and though Gordon and I slogged our way to 76 for the first wicket, Bishen Bedi found that the pitch would turn as well as seam. But a lead of 59 proved critical. Greenidge's greased reflexes brought him four catches close to the wicket and Bob Stephenson claimed three victims as our challengers crumbled to Mottram and O'Sullivan. There was nothing straightforward about the 90 we needed to win, but I survived a tantalising duel with Bedi to see us home inside two days. My 37 not out in 30 overs hardly offered any statistical satisfaction, but I regarded it as probably my best innings of the season.

Nottinghamshire's visit to Bournemouth later that week lasted less than two hours into the third day. Bottom of the table, their painfully fragile batting was cruelly exposed by our spin attack and impeccable close fielding. O'Sullivan had match figures that might have persuaded this dry character to start a scrapbook: 28·5 overs, 16 maidens, 41 runs, 11 wickets. Sainsbury's probing bowling picked up five of the others for only 11 runs and Nottinghamshire's 49 in their second innings was the second-lowest total of the summer.

Ironically we clinched the title against Gloucestershire, Prockie and all, beating them in a declaration match which at the time left ill feeling on their side. We did not need an outright victory; a collection of bonus points would make us champions. For their part a Gloucestershire win would ensure a place in the top four and some prize money. After Mike Taylor's 7 for 53 had brought us maximum bowling points, Gloucestershire's generous use of David Graveney and John Mortimore—their spin attack operated for all but 11 overs—helped us reach an eighth batting point which brought us, against all the pre-season betting, the County championship.

As they happily joined in our festivities, Gloucestershire expected a lessening of the pressure to help their cause. Instead only a protracted 170 from Sadiq Mohammed saved them from an innings defeat against our more grudging bowlers. In the end, Gloucestershire always struggled to make enough runs and Tony Brown had to declare with 9 wickets down to try for his win. Though we had already clinched the title, there was no question of our easing up, and we went on to make the 190 required in two hours. I don't think there has ever been any quarter given in matches between the two counties—always local rivals and this game certainly ensured that there would be no lessening of the rivalry—as was proved in the match which cost Gloucestershire the Championship in 1977. After participating in the winning of a Test series, every other cricket experience is an anticlimax, but though I could not muster a Derek Randall-style cartwheel when our winning point materialised I was extremely happy. Like all the team I was kicking myself for not having the confidence to gamble a few pounds when at the start of the season the bookmakers had categorised Hampshire as 66–1 outsiders.

Ten victories, an unbeaten season in the championship and an eventual margin of 31 points had made a mockery of those odds. The upset had its origins in our settled side with only thirteen players used and the regulars stimulated by the confidence of being automatic selections. The 71 catches shared by Gordon and myself will always be highlighted as the crucial department, and Gordon's maturing strokeplay which relegated me to second place in the averages for the first time built many a foundation on which our remarkable attack could flourish.

Just why the championship victory was not the first of three still remains unfathomable. For the 1974 side did not have to rely so extensively on that mystifying penetration from our unheralded attack. For myself the signing of Andy Roberts came as a disappointment—not that I held anything against the tall West Indian from Antigua. Though he had spent our championship summer in Hampshire's 2nd XI, I had never seen him bowl. But to sign Andy as an overseas player the county had to release Dave O'Sullivan. That particular debate gave captain and committee many hours of soul-searching, because Sully's 47 wickets in only 13 matches had proved a basic ingredient in our winning recipe. From my own point of view he had also been a tremendous social boost to the dressing-room.

By this time I had made an outlay on a house on the outskirts of Southampton; Sully and Mike Hill, the reserve wicket-keeper, completed the household, where attempts at domesticity were restricted to washing-up and garbage disposal at infrequent intervals. Though I was not sensitive to it at the time, Dave could have hardly relished Mike's continual complaining that Andy Roberts's lightning pace was for ever bruising his hands.

At the end of the 1973 season Richard Gilliat asked my opinion on which of the two bowlers should be retained. Although I was on the selection committee, I felt I could not give an objective view. Reluctantly, but wisely as events would prove, the county gave Sully his cards and since then his appearances in this country have been restricted to the Minor Counties and the Leagues.

The effect of the unveiling of Andy Roberts on both the reputation and person of county batsmen resembled the devastation of a tornado. For the first month of the season the only word I heard him utter was 'Coke' in reply to an invitation for a drink—except of course for the roared appeals. And there were plenty of those, most of which were upheld. Six times he took more than 5 wickets in an innings, including 8 for 46 against Glamorgan; he topped the first-class averages with 119 wickets at a cost of only 13·62 each; all but 8 of that haul came in the championship and he was first in the country past the hundred mark. In a much publicised incident he rushed a bouncer past the elegant hook of Colin Cowdrey, hitting him on the head and adding to the great man's indignity by toppling him on to his wicket. The 2nd XI had joyously reported to us the gory details of a match when Gloucestershire were 200 for 2 with Nos. 8 and 9 at the wicket because Andy's speed had induced a succession of retirements, and now that unlikely event needed no explanation.

And yet we did not retain our title. Again a remarkable freedom from injury meant that only thirteen players appeared in the championship; again we won ten matches though this time three were lost. But the elements, and one particular lapse on the field, conspired against us. The lapse occurred at Cardiff in the third week in August where Glamorgan, who were to finish ingloriously in sixteenth place, somehow beat us by 5 wickets; yet they had trailed by 144 runs in the first innings after Roberts had turned in the best performance of his career. I hope Len Hill will forgive me, but his match-winning 90 was the worst score of that magnitude I have ever seen, a complete block for just under six hours. Peter Sainsbury bowled 63 overs for 73 runs in the second innings! The points that wriggled from our grasp that day would have eliminated the misfortune of the dreadful weather which finally thwarted us.

The final dramas were enacted at Bournemouth, where Yorkshire were to be our last opponents of the season, and at Chelmsford, where Worcestershire, who had tagged us for most of the season, were chasing points against Essex. Although rain fell heavily throughout the country over the three days, there were enough clear intervals to beat us.

At Chelmsford play was possible on the Saturday. In 14 overs Norman Gifford took 7 for 15, but his greater contribution was in winning the toss and putting in Essex. Had Worcestershire batted, the weather and the difficult conditions when play was possible might well have frustrated their attempts to gain the three bonus points they needed to inch in front of Hampshire. As it was, their full four bowling points gave them a two-point lead at the end of the first day.

That is the way it stayed, and not a solitary ball was bowled at Bournemouth. It must have been similarly nail-biting for the Worcester lads, because the second and third days of their game were also washed out. A less classic duel you would find hard to depict; two teams feet up in the dressing-room with one ear on the radio reports from the other ground and the other on the sound of the rainfall.

In 1975 nothing could have been more blameless than the weather. In this World Cup summer, cricket grounds turned brown under skies that were more native to Port Elizabeth than to Portsmouth. We had been losing semi-finalists in the Benson & Hedges and quarter-finalists in the Gillette Cup, and desperately wanted to regain the championship even though it seemed likely we would win the John Player title. An injury as unusual as it was unexpected finally exposed the friendliness of our attack on the beautiful batting wickets produced by the dry summer.

Against Sussex at Southampton, Gordon Greenidge played the highest innings by a Hampshire batsman since the war: 259 runs fashioned with brutal power, including 13 sixes, a championship record. Andy Roberts, now nearing the end of his third county season, had begun to show reaction to the overbowling which followed his initial impact. As Sussex came out to begin their reply to our 501 for 5, Andy broke down during his practice run-up.

We did enforce the follow-on, but only because Sussex could not score quickly enough within the limit of 100 overs. Then followed what seemed like an eternity in the field as they amassed 524 in their second innings. Mark Faber, an exciting stroke player on his day, but not a batsman you would expect to play a big innings, found our bowling of such little inconvenience that he scored 176; Groome, Hoadley and Mansell, hardly names you would look for at the top of the averages, all passed 50; John Spencer, arriving when the game had been saved, helped himself to 79 in twenty-five minutes.

Worse was to follow. John Ward of Derbyshire faced us in the next match in such terrible form that he had already decided to retire from the game. But though he walked to the wicket for their second innings averaging around 13, he too found survival no problem and finished with a maiden first-class century. Ward and Alan Hill (no relative to the aforementioned Len but a brother in spirit) held us at bay for five hours. Without that extra cutting edge of Roberts our attack just could not find a way past the bats of those who were bent only on occupying the crease.

Neither Hill nor John Ward were in the Derbyshire side earlier that same week when a victory in the picturesque setting of Darley Dale ensured that our cupboard would not be entirely bare. This time Hampshire were to head Worcestershire by two points at the top of the John Player League, our 13 wins in 16 matches equalling the best for the competition. I do remember batting in that match—one of my few Sunday League reminiscences—when Alan Ward bowled the sort of poor length and generous width that Gordon and I really appreciated. Seven an over for 14 overs flowed before we were parted. My 52 enabled me to set a new standard for a season's work on Sundays—an achievement, together with our outright win, which at least removed some of my general dissatisfaction with the principle of playing on Sundays.

Even allowing for the two trophies and for the extra inducement of being in at the kill in a number of sprints for victory, I still found my struggles were more inward than outward, but not until 1977 did I ever feel that I was not giving Hampshire value for money. After Gordon's splurge of runs in 1973 and his recognition as a world-class batsman, I still returned to the top of the championship averages for the next three seasons. But the battle of self-motivation grew progressively tougher. There were still days when the smoothness reappeared—for instance the 225 not out against Nottinghamshire at Trent Bridge in 1974, when I carried my bat out of a total of 344—but demands for intensive spells of concentration became harder to bear. Contrary to a popular school of thought, off-days are never planned; I have never tossed away my wicket for the relief of a rest in the pavilion. Rather I can only cope with playing every day by batting in a carefree style—but not a careless one.

Those who are kind enough to make excuses for my disillusionment always point to the South African situation. A regular dose of Test cricket, they say, would have acted like a tonic. That may be a valid point. I would also add that the limited range of distractions and relaxations in the Southampton area have made it hard to find a life outside cricket. Without a wife or a family, the tiresome aspects of the day are not so easily forgotten. Perhaps I could have unwound to a greater extent in a big-city atmosphere. Certainly the twelve-month-a-year involvement in cricket all over the world has been going far too long when a love has become a chore.

It saddens me when I think of my breathless excitement at walking out to play for Hampshire for the first time. Suddenly I had really become a part of those cricket books I had read with such intensity as I grew up in Durban. Now I don't read them any more. And I know that when I walk off a county ground for the last time—whenever that may be—it will be with an enormous sense of relief.

Chapter 11

Currie Cup Challenge

My early days at Hampshire, where I saw at close quarters the problems of leading players who were earning their livelihood from the game, brought one resolve. I was determined that I would never accept an appointment to captain professionals. But, with the possible exception of my truncated Test career, nothing has given me more satisfaction than leading the amateurs of Natal in the Currie Cup.

Not for one minute do I suppose that I was the natural choice for the convenor Derek Dowling. For years the captaincy of the province had been an on-the-field position, to guide ten other names handed over by the selectors. Those names had varied so much that in one season twenty-three players had represented the 'A' side in the eight Currie Cup matches. I represented a threat to the old order, because I made it clear that I would only lead out a side that I had had a say in selecting; yet Natal's lack of success had become so acute that I was appointed for the 1973-74 season.

After seven successive wins in the 1960s (including a tie with Transvaal in 1966), there had been such a decline that rival provinces now looked upon us as walking bonus points. I returned from my season with South Australia into a side in a transitional phase; constant disappointing performances had ripped holes in the confidence of the players.

In 1971, however, it was not this lack of success that almost led to my defection to Northern Transvaal. Once again I felt I had to make a positive reaction to an offer which made financial sense in the insecure world of professional cricket. In Natal we were not strictly amateur; but a match fee of 10 rand per game, plus another 10 rand for winning, hardly offered the prospect of a secure old age.

I didn't really want to leave, particularly because Northern Transvaal played in the 'B' section, but there seemed little alternative. In one last attempt to save my career in my home state, I approached Derek Dowling with the details of the offer in the hope that he might come some way towards matching it. I was quite mortified at his reply: 'My advice is for you to accept it. There's no way we can match that.'

Not for the first time in my life, Les Theobald came to the rescue. For not entirely philanthropic reasons—he wanted me for his Durban High School Old Boys' side—he mustered enough guarantors, all private individuals who produced sums from 200 to 1,000 rand, to give me a contract. After the shattering let-down of Natal's reaction, I was thrilled at the response to Theo's initiative. Within a few days this personal sponsorship was formalised into an entirely new enterprise, the Kingsmead Mynahs Club, which employed me and later other professionals to co-ordinate coaching in Natal. I happily signed for three years. Later Clover Dairies would add their sponsorship, giving me the incentive of 2 rand per run at home, and half that in away matches where the publicity was of lesser value to the company.

I actually led Natal for the first time in the last three matches of the 1971–72 season, when Pat Trimborn went down with injury. Though I had a very enjoyable season with the bat, passing the milestone of the first player to score a thousand runs in a Currie Cup year, I hardly waved a winning wand over the team. One and a half days after I tossed the coin for the first time we were on our way home from Port Elizabeth.

With Peter Pollock, Sibley McAdam and Tony Greig, Eastern Province had all the equipment to exploit a wet wicket. I made the wrong call at the toss, Graeme Pollock invited us to bat and we were beaten by 10 wickets. It's a match that Greiggy will never forget, because in the second innings he set up a trap into which I tumbled. For McAdam, he dropped down to backward square-leg on the fence to counteract the pick-up shot off my legs which I used to play frequently. When I had only made 1, Sibley pitched the perfect delivery for the plan. I picked it high off my toes. Greiggy didn't have to move six inches to make the catch. After tossing the ball two hundred feet in the air in triumph, he then set off on a lap of honour, racing round the batsman's wicket before leaping on the bowler with an enormous hug. Reticence has never been Tony's problem.

I was in charge for another defeat, at Prockie's hands in Bulawayo—a match in which Dennis Gamsy received his retribution for a career of optimistic appealing; he and Trimmie had perfected the appeal in unison which often swayed the umpire into an error of judgement, in a similar style to the Welsh choir of Glamorgan's Malcolm Nash and Eifion Jones. This time Gamsy was given out caught in the gulley when the ball had come off his boot, and then adjudged lbw when his front leg was a mile down the wicket. Each time Prockie looked up at the sky and commented: 'Yup, the man up there has got you.'

The man up there certainly cast no benevolent gazes in the direction of Natal; with ample time to make just over 200 to win we fell 20-odd short. Ritchie Kaschula, a useful slow left-armer but the most unathletic fielder I have seen in my cricket career—you could take a single to him at silly mid-on—took three important wickets. By the strange points system of the competition, a win over Transvaal in our final match would have brought us the Currie Cup. In fact we were one wicket short of that victory at the close and so finished fourth out of five.

By the standards of the following year, with André Bruyns as captain, that had been a triumphant season. In 1972–73 we became the team that the other provinces loved to play–winning just one match and finishing bottom of the table. Promising though they were, youngsters like Henry Fotheringham and Darryl Bestall were still in the infancy of their careers. I remember Henry's first confrontation with Prockie, who quickly sensed that the youngster was happiest on the front foot. The predictable response was a bouncer which a shaken Fotheringham just lobbed over short leg off his glove. 'Try and drive that, you little schoolboy,' was the accompanying comment.

I did manage to pass the thousand mark for a second time, but perhaps the season's two most enjoyable matches were against the Derrick Robins XI. Their strong party included Bob Willis, John Lever, Jackie Hampshire, Frank Hayes and John Murray, and they beat Natal only in a thrilling finish when Hayes in near-darkness picked out van der Bijl's last ball of the match and slammed it for the winning boundary. In a mini-Test our Invitation XI had the satisfaction of an innings victory, though once again I managed to lose my wicket immediately after reaching three figures.

That season ended in controversy when a dispute over playing regulations denied Rhodesia a win against Eastern Province which would have ensured outright victory in the Currie Cup. In the last session of play, with Rhodesia batting towards success, the umpires apparently changed their minds about the time when the last hour of play, with its statutory 20 overs, had begun; that simple operation had been complicated by a stoppage for drinks within the period. Lorrie Wilmot, the Eastern Province captain, understood that the first over before the refreshment break began the last 20; all Rhodesia believed that the full allocation started after the stoppage.

Nineteen overs after the resumption Prockie's side needed 6 runs to win with 4 wickets left and with the captain 66 not out and in complete control. Suddenly Wilmot led his side from the field and, despite entreaties from both umpires, refused to return because he was sure the full number of overs had been bowled. At the time the match was awarded by default to Rhodesia, but this was subsequently quashed and the final verdict was a draw. Bitterly upset, the Rhodesian officials ordered the making of a replica of the Currie Cup and presented it to Prockie. To complicate matters even further, Transvaal, Eastern Province and Western Province all finished with 84 points, but by virtue of the most outright wins Transvaal were champions. Rhodesia, champions in their own minds, were officially fourth.

You could have got long odds against Natal succeeding Transvaal. Even the newly appointed captain was uncertain, but I was determined to stimulate some sort of improvement. I asked the selectors if I could pick a team and tell those players that they would be given more than one chance to prove themselves; morale had been in a wheelspin following the persistent switching of the line-up. Though several officials, probably correctly, held grave misgivings about my sense of diplomacy, they backed me; and from the team I could have asked for no greater support.

I suppose I began with their respect because of my achievements in first-class cricket; the problem as a captain was not to lose it through mistakes on the field. A relationship I developed with one of the side helped dispel that worry. In the previous seasons, the penetration of our seam bowlers, van der Bijl, Trimborn and Aubrey Lilley, had been wasted because the spin attack had been unable to take further wickets or to contain the opposition while the pacemen had their rest.

Pelham Henwood, our slow left-arm bowler, came into this category. He was lucky to be playing at all, lucky in fact to be alive. Driving one night in a Mini along a farm road he came to a 'T' junction which was not signposted; at sixty miles an hour his car dropped thirty feet off the built-up road, nose-diving on to the bonnet; on impact one shinbone shot up and shattered a kneecap. Walking seemed unlikely, let alone bowling.

Courageously, he made his way back into cricket, and I devised a style of attack for him which was completely different from the methods which had brought him only sporadic success in the past. I got him to bowl at the leg stump, to the type of leg-side field that I had seen used successfully in one-day cricket in England—a short-leg, one man at 45 degrees, another for the lap, a mid-wicket and a mid-on. Not only did his haul of wickets improve, he was rarely struck for more than 2 runs an over.

In all senses, he was a man revitalised, and he was voted one of the five South African Cricketers of the Year at the end of 1973–74 season. One incident, in particular, may have cemented the necessary confidence between bowler and captain. Against Eastern Province I sensed that Lorrie Wilmot was getting frustrated; I moved one fielder three-quarters of the way back to the fence and suggested to Pelly he should float the next delivery a little higher. Wilmot obliged by slogging it straight down the fielder's throat.

Vince van der Bijl and 'Tich' Smith, the wicket-keeper, my two closest friends, were a tremendous help on the field. Both are the sort of player I really feel sorry for, because they have worked so hard at their cricket and they will never play at the Test level that their talents and efforts deserve. Mind you, from time to time I could have strangled Vince on the field because he wouldn't bowl a bouncer at a troublesome opponent. 'Jeez, Barry, I'd kill him' was a reasoning I found hard to break down.

Later in the season Natal acquired the services of Bob Woolmer, who stayed on after the Derrick Robins tour. I wanted him in the side, but the committee approached him without my knowledge and, in fact, offered him more money than the sum he would have come for. I am sure that his seasons in South Africa helped him develop into a Test player, particularly in his batting, which had been very restricted in the Kent side because he regularly went in as low as No. 8.

In my three years as the appointed captain, Natal lost only three Currie Cup matches. In the light of my record when I deputised for Trimborn, you won't be surprised to learn that the first defeat came in my very first match against Western Province —a tactical catastrophe! I was trying to be clever over the new bonus points structure, and I declared our first innings, when I could have batted on, because we could gain no more extra points. Eddie Barlow had invited Natal to bat and I had taken great delight in making 186 not out. But because of my impetuous declaration Eddie was laughing at the end.

Our only genuine piece of misfortune in that match came when Fred Goldstein was given not out at 0 when a ball from Lilley brushed his gloves on the way to the wicketkeeper; Goldstein finished with 104 and his side with a lead of 90. In barely more than one session of play our second innings crumbled to 130 all out. Barlow took the points, while I got nothing but a panning in the press.

I have never been the 'well played' type and I took the defeat badly, recognising my own shortcomings which had thrown away the advantage of our first innings. Fortunately after two draws against Rhodesia and Transvaal we got off the mark with an innings win over Eastern Province at Kingsmead. I was indebted to a dropped catch by Chris Wilkins off Rupert Hanley when I had made only 1; my 152 gave the innings a focal point, but I felt we had turned the corner away from inconsistency, since our lowest score of the innings was Woolmer's 24.

Vince produced a magnificent spell of bowling—12 for 85 in the match—to bring us a handsome 221-run revenge victory over Western Province, and bonus points at Port Elizabeth lifted us to the top of the table for the first time with one match to play. It was a finish with almost excessive spice. An outright win for Transvaal or Natal would take the trophy; in the event of a draw we needed six bonus points to inch ahead of Western Province; Transvaal would have to make nine and restrict us to win in those circumstances. The extra twist in the drama was our pairing in the Gillette Cup final a week before the Currie Cup contest.

Transvaal struck the first psychological blow, and won the Gillette Cup. In a thrilling encounter Natal ended up 10 runs short, thereby not spoiling the last appearance at the Wanderers of Ali Bacher and Don Mackay-Coghill, who were carried shoulder-high from the field at the end. For the second successive season we fell short of the knockout cup; the previous year Eastern Province's players had been offered 500 rand if they dismissed me for less than 20. At 18 I hit a four and smilingly apologised to the close fielders; with the incentive removed I got out to the next ball, the worst delivery of the match and certainly the worst shot. Worse still, I think they got their bonus anyway!

But at Kingsmead, Bacher had nothing like Trevor Goddard's perfect finish to his first-class career. An imperious cover drive by Bob Woolmer, right in the style of his mentor Colin Cowdrey, brought Natal the vital sixth bonus point. Now only a Transvaal win could deny us, but as 'Tich' Smith extended our first innings with an invaluable 87, their prospects receded. I could not have been more gratified when Pelham Henwood demolished their second innings to give us the added sparkle of an outright win. My own batting had broken further domestic records, but I took most pride in Pelly's triumph; his figures on that last afternoon were 32 overs, 17 maidens, 34 runs, 7 wickets.

My catch-phrase at our regular team meeting before the start of play had become a joke with the team. Every day I would say 'This is the day we are going to win it.' As we whooped our way through the celebrations I didn't need their continual reminding that this indeed was the day.

The real stimulation of captaincy had come in the field; in the past we had allowed the opposition to wriggle out of trouble and set us targets that were beyond our means. That season we did not let it slip, even though I had to learn very quickly how to bring out the best in each individual. In that respect I had been well taught by the example of Ian Chappell, the best captain I have ever played under; he always knew who needed to be handled gently and who would respond to a good bawling-out.

I almost made a mistake with Henry Fotheringham, who is very sensitive. As the junior member of the side he naturally became the butt of the humour of the senior players; on one occasion I was persuaded to go along with a gag. As captain I had a special corner of the dressing-room for changing; innocent Henry was told that he could use that area. On cue I arrived, threw a pretended fit of temper and told him to shift his gear immediately. While the rest of the team fought personal battles to keep a straight face Henry got really upset. 'If this is what playing in the "A" side is all about, I'm not playing,' he yelled. It took me months to convince him that it was a joke.

Of course sometimes the joke was on me. My dislike of gallons of juice around the inevitable fruit salad at lunchtime was well known. One day Pete Albers, a fine cricketer with enormous hands, fetched my sweet for me and came back with a bowl that was brimming with juice. I took one look and started swearing and yelling 'Don't you know I can't stand the stuff', and so on. He just picked up the fruit in a lump, made as if to wring it out and threw it back on the table, while the rest of the team collapsed in hysteria.

We went through the 1974-75 season unbeaten, but we missed retaining the Currie Cup by one point. Once again Natal met Transvaal in a final match of almost unfathomable complexity. Once again Western Province, their programme complete, held the lead, but a win plus a haul of bonus points from either side would see them caught. I reached the fastest century of the season —by an odd quirk taking that award from Trevor Jesty, who was playing for Griqualand West—in 103 minutes to see us to victory, but we fell short by one bonus point.

In certain ways it typified a frustrating season. Twice I had gone against my better judgement and allowed myself to become embroiled in arguments with umpires, though on both occasions I know I was in the right. The first incident concerned a run-out against Eastern Province at Port Elizabeth. Dave Brickett was bowling to me without a mid-off, and as I drove him through the gap I knew I would safely make 3 runs. For the third run I would be running to the bowler's end, the danger end nearer to the fielder, Simon Bezuidenhout. My partner, Dave Dyer, was concentrating on Simon and didn't hear my call at first, but finally saw I was running and set off for the wicketkeeper's end. The throw came to the bowler's end where Robbie Muzzell instinctively took the bails off, though I was in, but immediately sensed that Dave was struggling to make his ground. A brilliant throw hit the stumps and Dave was out by a couple of feet.

That would have been the end of the matter had not the umpire at my end been spotted by Lorrie Wilmot. In response to Robbie's automatic appeal against me he had tentatively raised his finger then pulled it down again when Dave had been given out. Lorrie sensed the chance of claiming my wicket, so he told Graeme Pollock, the Eastern Province captain, what he had observed. They confronted the umpire, a gentleman named Murray who was umpiring his first 'A' section match, and he finally admitted he had given me out. By this time Dave Dyer was back in the dressing room with his pads off. I refused to go because I knew I had been in by a yard; by now Mr Murray did not know what he had to do, so he called over the other umpire, Sandy Matthews, and finally I was given out. Dave was called back to resume his innings.

But even that incredible piece of umpiring paled in comparison with the events against Western Province at Newlands. After gaining a lead of 50 on the first innings, we were mounting a real attempt to win the match. Jack Nel opened their second knock with Eddie Barlow, and in Vince's second or third over he cut a delivery back into Nel; via his pad, then his bat, the ball lobbed into the covers, where Gerald Katz held a simple catch. We didn't even bother to appeal, but Nel stood there and umpire Van Gendt said 'Not out.'

I rushed up to him and asked him how he thought the ball could have travelled thirty yards off his pad, at which point he said that Vince had blocked his view and he had not seen the catch completed. There was a simple answer to that: consult the square-leg umpire. Mr van Gendt declined to do so and ordered us to restart play.

Nel immediately took a single which brought Barlow to face. Off the very next ball he fenced outside the off stump and nicked an obvious catch to 'Tich' Smith. Eddie, to whom walking is as palatable as water to an alcoholic, stood his ground; again the decision went against us. In three deliveries we had been denied the wickets of two opening batsmen at a crucial stage of our season. In the folklore of the game, the next delivery is supposed to tear out the middle stump, followed by sarcastic appeals of 'How was *that*?' Vince nearly managed it. The next delivery ripped back into Barlow off the pitch and trapped him plumb in front. When Mr van Gendt responded to the beseeching appeal with a raised finger, I collapsed in a mock faint and waved my cap at him. In such traditional circles I was, of course, reprimanded, and I did apologise.

We did not end the season empty-handed. Two inspired pieces of cricket by van der Bijl helped us win the Gillette Cup for the first time. His bold 26, including an enormous six off Stephen Jones, stretched our innings to respectable proportions; then at deep fine-leg he clung on to a hook to dismiss Barlow for 1; Western Province never got back on the rails after that.

Though I would lead Natal to another victory in the Currie Cup the following season, I gave my detractors—and in South Africa I have many because they don't appreciate my attitude to my profession—more scope for criticism. Together with Graeme Pollock and Lee Irvine, I refused to play in the first representative game against the International Wanderers. The issue, naturally, was one of money. Our request was for the same pay as the International players; I didn't mind Dennis Lillee trying to knock my head off—that's part and parcel of the game—but I felt I deserved to earn the same as the bowler for a spectacle that would pull the crowds through the gates. The spectator, I thought, wouldn't react quite as positively to a confrontation between Lillee and, say, Clive Rice or 'Tich' Smith.

I made my request six weeks before the tourists arrived. Nevertheless, the final offer was of 900 rand for the three-game series when I knew that the opposition would receive in the region of 2,500 rand per man. Eddie Barlow had been appointed captain for the series so his copybook was not for blotting, but Graeme, Lee and I took a stand that I still believe was right.

Of course I didn't handle the matter with kid gloves, and I will admit that some of the resulting bad publicity was again due to my lack of tact. I was accused of rocking the boat when a multiracial series was being established. I was sent telegrams from parents whose sons were fighting on the border for three rand a day. I was refused admission when the Johannesburg *Sunday Times* sent me to Newlands to cover the match from which I had stood down. And Dick Lambert, who was running the Kingsmead Mynahs, spoke out publicly without my knowledge, saying that he would order me to play in the second game because it was in my contract to that club.

All three of us decided we had made our stand and did make ourselves available for the second game. In fact, without us the South African Invitation XI had more than held their own until Gary Gilmour, batting virtually one-handed after a shoulder injury, struck 80 in 64 minutes in a desperate but successful bid to lift his side out of trouble. Against Alan Hurst, John Shepherd and Ashley Mallett, the South Africans stumbled to 69 all out and defeat by 185 runs.

Thankfully all of us justified our selection for the second match, though we received no extra payment as a result of our 'strike'. Graeme played in his very best form to score 124, Lee made 30 in both innings and I rattled up 52 in the first knock, though Lillee had me caught behind in the second for 0. But we staved off defeat and in the third match, at Kingsmead, levelled the series.

The match was a triumph for the non-whites because Babu Ebrahim, one of the three SACBOC members who played in each of the games, bowled us to victory, taking 6 for 66 with his slow left-arm spin. Such representation of the non-white members had been a condition of the tour, and Tiffi Barnes, Pinki Carelse, Howie Bergins and Farokh Timol had all been given the opportunity to play against opponents of the calibre of Dennis Lillee, Greg Chappell, Glen Turner, Max Walker and Derek Underwood. For cricket reasons alone Eric Rowan had been very much against their inclusion, but though Babu might never become one of the great bowlers of all time, the day he won the game for 'South Africa' was another step towards the end of our exile.

I finished the match with a sore head, the after-effects of a blow from Alan Hurst in our second innings. I had played one or two shots off him to reach 70, and he let me know his opinion with two successive bouncers. His style is not to bowl a good length but to bowl it either full or short. I don't think I expected the third bouncer in succession. As I began to duck I was shocked to see that instead of lifting over my head, the ball was scooting off the track. Instinctively I turned away, but I was hit behind the ear, where one's balance is controlled, so that I had to wobble back to the pavilion. After a night in hospital under observation, Eddie ordered me back to the middle again, but I felt poorly and I only added another 10 runs.

That was only the third time in my career that I have been hit on the head. The first, ironically, came from Prockie's bowling on a slow pitch at Bristol: he switched to attack me round the wicket, and I knew what was coming. Unfortunately, I went through the shot too soon and I took the blow on the temple; it was lights out. After being struck by a former team-mate, the second occasion concerned a player who afterwards joined forces with me. Richard Elms spent the 1977 season with Hampshire, but four years earlier he sent me back to South Africa in the most uncomfortable way. In my last innings of the 1973 season against Kent at Southampton Gordon and I had put on 240; Richard then totally surprised me with a bouncer which I top-edged into my face. I discharged myself from hospital and endured the journey back to Durban with a depressed fracture of the cheekbone.

Before Hurst struck me I had retired once earlier in that season, in our first Currie Cup match in Bulawayo; after batting for most of our first innings to make 159 and then fielding, I collapsed with heat exhaustion at 69 not out. But the season had its more humorous moments, like batting left-handed to Prockie's left-arm bowling as we easily beat Rhodesia in Durban; and getting out to a slow full-toss delivered by John Stephenson, the Eastern Province wicket-keeper who was filling in as makeshift bowler; and a mid-season flying visit to New Zealand, where I partnered John Snow in the Wellington Centenary Double Wicket competition and of course had to bowl into the gale-force winds of the most blustery city in the southern hemisphere.

Though Western Province's Denys Hobson bowled us out twice in little more than a day to bring us to a second defeat of the season —Stephenson's switch to bowling had helped Eastern Province to a 9-wicket win—we ended as champions to really complete our revival from those dismal performances of earlier years. Our last game, with the title already settled, was once again the traditional meeting with Transvaal, and a finale for Pat Trimborn, another cricketer whose name will be easily forgotten because his Test career was cut short by politics. In the midst of a reception for Pat I remarked to Vince that I too might have played my last game for Natal.

The treatment of Trimmie reminded me once again that loyal service is not a quality that administrators appreciate. After seventeen years, the latter part of which was spent bowling in pain after a serious knee operation, Natal saw fit to present him with a mounted cricket ball. Because the likes of Roy McLean and Jackie McGlew had never received a cent for their loyalty, the officials, steeped in the philosophy of amateurism, would not bend. An ex-gratia payment of 1,000 rand would really have been peanuts in terms of Trimmie's devotion to Natal cricket, but it might have helped cover the cost of his operation.

Two other factors made me look elsewhere for my cricket. The main one was that I was growing stale of the repetition of the Currie Cup circuit, a similar reaction to my feelings about county cricket. For all the excitement of contributing to Natal's rise from a bunch of also-rans to a winning side, the pressure on my personal performance was beginning to tell. Secondly, there had been a change in my personal life: on a brief trip to Australia to play in a charity match for spastics, I had met a beautiful girl called Shelley Sullivan.

So in every sense I welcomed an opportunity to return to Australia for a season's cricket. Dennis Tobin, a contact from my previous visits, in conjunction with Keith Slater, who had played for Australia against England in 1959, passed on to me an offer from the Midland-Guildford club in Perth. I discussed the matter with Vince and 'Tich' Smith and they could see no reason why I should not accept it; as they said, I had no real ties in South Africa.

That was not strictly true. My parents still remained in Durban, but they saw the benefits of the move. With my father I had also established business interests in the property market. Through the wise counsel of Alec Thompson and the financial aid of Alec Savage, we had taken my savings out of building societies and invested in buildings. I now have two blocks of flats in the city, and my father handles the occupancies. As long as every apartment is rented we make a small profit, and the whole enterprise has helped to rectify some of the insecurity I have always been troubled by since I accepted a life as a professional sportsman.

But since my father could handle the business, and would enjoy it, I decided to ask Natal for my release from the final year of a second third-year contract. I didn't realise how pleased they would be to see me go. Neither before nor after the formal release did I receive a letter from anybody in Natal asking me to reconsider. Perhaps they had heard me too often criticising the paltry presentations given to other players, but there was never even a suggestion of a commemorative dinner. In the five seasons since my sabbatical in South Australia, I had hardly left a South African batting record untouched; their lack of appreciation explains why I am now so cynical about figures. Despite the merry-go-round of players within the provinces, I had never deserted the place where I learned the game.

I do hope that there is a silent majority among the public who have enjoyed my contribution to Natal cricket, but I have rarely received any letters except the usual requests for autographs. One honourable exception is Monica Graham, a charming lady who lives in Rhodesia, who always remembers my birthday and who has made special trips to Durban and to Johannesburg to see me play.

My one regret was leaving behind my team-mates—a bunch of tremendous fellows—but I could have recommended no greater replacement than Prockie, who was signed from Rhodesia. I wished him luck on my way through South Africa to start my season in Perth. At the same time I realised once again how much I was looking forward to a quiet season encouraging youngsters in grade cricket.

Not until I had a phone call from the agents of Kerry Packer did I realise just how quiet I would have to be.

Chapter 12

'Piracy' Under Packer

Tony Greig was convinced that I was responsible for the first public revelations about what is now generally known as Kerry Packer's circus. Throughout the early months of 1977 the world's leading cricketers had been approached with a secrecy which would have impressed any undercover agent. A key part of the planning involved a dramatic announcement of the *fait accompli* later in the year.

But on April 24th, Lee Irvine stood up to thank a dinner gathering in Johannesburg to mark his retirement from first-class cricket. In the course of his speech he surprised the audience by referring to four South African cricketers who had 'signed lucrative contracts to play an eight-week series of matches throughout the world'. The players were, correctly, named as Eddie Barlow, Mike Procter, Graeme Pollock and myself.

Greig immediately supposed that it was I who had sprung the leak because of my close friendship with Lee; others in on the secret must have suspected the same. But I had never spoken a word about the operation except to those I knew were already on the inside. I can only assume that Lee stumbled across the information because in South Africa similar plans were afoot for the sponsorship of an unofficial 'South African XI' to play against the rest of the world. Any potential sponsor checking on the availability of leading South African players might easily have been alerted to the non-availability of some and the reasons for it.

However he found out, Lee's revelations were finally picked upon by the world's press to make public this enormous upheaval of the traditional structure of cricket. Since I had signed a contract two months earlier, at the beginning of March, I was glad when the barrier of silence was finally lifted, just as I was glad that I had been able to take one last opportunity to end my ostracism from playing with and against cricketers of the very highest calibre.

I signed for Kerry Packer in the Parmelia Hotel in Perth, though I had not actually met the man himself at the time. The approach came from an agency called JP Sports, the 'J' referring to John Cornell, the 'P' to Paul Hogan, the Australian television personality; a third member of their organisation who made the first contact on the telephone was Austen Robertson, who made a name for himself as a star Australian Rules player.

At the first meeting the whole revolutionary aspect of the affair made me cautious; there was no mention of the name of Packer either, just acknowledgements to a wealthy and influential backer. Even though the amount of money I was offered was a real eye-opener—as much as I could earn at Hampshire in three seasons—I asked for time to consider the implications of siding with an organisation that was so unofficial.

For advice I turned to Ross Edwards, the former Australian Test batsman, who had already been approached by JP Sports. An accountant, Ross had studied the entire deal with a business acumen that was beyond me, and his positive conclusion influenced my decision in favour of the deal. With no Test career to put in jeopardy I had less to lose than many of the others who had been approached; my main concern remained my benefit with Hampshire that year, but I was assured that my county contract would be unaffected and that I would be free to play the entire English summer.

In fact I became one of the first to pledge my allegiance. There was no negotiation about terms; it was very much a 'take it or leave it' philosophy. I took it, and signed up for three years. I had still not met Kerry Packer. He wasn't present either at another secret assignation at London's Churchill Hotel on the evening of Easter Monday. But Procter, Pollock, Barlow, Knott, Underwood, Snow and Greig were, and I began to appreciate the magnitude of the operation.

I finally met him at length the following June after a phone call asking my opinion of the merits of Gordon Greenidge. I told them that he ought to be part of the circus because he is a world-class player, and Gordon and I were invited to another rendez-vous. One evening during the Surrey-Hampshire match at Guildford we met in London, and Gordon eventually signed as well. Packer has been painted as a man who has had a Svengali effect on those he has approached; an exaggeration maybe, but there is no doubt that he knows what he wants and he is used to getting his way.

As I have said before, the sheer opportunity of another 'test' series, however unofficial, earned my support; many others, with more caps than a schoolboy outfitters', could not afford to turn down the money. But in the endless debates that followed the unveiling of the project, the actual participants have been branded as villainous as the two principals, Packer himself and Tony Greig.

I must stress that I am writing at a time when the High Court is still deliberating over the issue, and there is still much to be decided. I must also stress that I do understand those who support the traditional structure of the game—after all my own career is a product of that style of organization. Like any cricket-lover I hope the matter can be speedily resolved and that the game does not suffer. Nevertheless, to many of the public we are simply a battalion of mercenaries and Greiggy is the king of the money-grabbers. As captain of England at the time, his defection has been labelled the worst since Judas Iscariot's. But until the intervention of Packer precipitated the TCCB to accept sponsorship at Test match level, which put more remuneration into the pockets of the international players, you couldn't pay a bill by writing a note which said 'But I am captain of England.'

I don't malign Greig at all. For all the controversy, he has injected life into English cricket, which was a corpse after the mauling in Australia in 1974-75. Whatever he has done, good or bad, he has got people talking about the game; he has been walking publicity for cricket, more so than any other player for many years. But, had he not taken this chance of a secure future for himself, his wife and his children, he would have run the risk of an income which faded as time eroded his talents. At thirty-five or forty no one would be paying him for all the valuable service he had given the game, nor for all the youngsters he had attracted to the sport. Weighing up the pros and cons of the Packer approach, he could only come to one decision.

Even those who see the merit in the plan have been critical of the methods used, and have speculated about the real reasons for Kerry Packer's actions. Why he became involved has never really been in dispute. As a television magnate, he wanted to use the series to bargain for the television contract in Australia for his station, Channel Nine, to screen exclusively the conventional Test matches. Cricket, if you like, was just a means to his end; but his ambition has benefited certain players. The salaries of international cricketers have been restricted owing to traditional policy within the game; the revenue from Test matches and television rights are spread right down to grassroots level. The spread has been so wide that the performers themselves have been left with small reward for staging the spectacle which produces the funds. For many years the difference in income between the journeyman county pro and the regular Test star has been marginal. It was that chink in the system which Packer exploited.

Why, critics have asked, didn't Packer approach Lord's first of all? Probably he imagined a chilly reception to a request to sanction a series with the world's top fifty players? Why, then, did he not wait for that inevitable rejection before setting up his unofficial organisation? Because, forewarned, the authorities could have acted to legislate against the move before it got off the ground. Arriving with the contracts for fifty players in his hand, he felt, gave him the strength to negotiate.

Of course, apart from any other influence I am sure that the circus immediately hurried through a better deal for Test players when the deal with Cornhill Insurance upped the fee for playing for England to £1,000; I find it hard to believe that the same improvements would have happened if there had been no threat of players defecting to Packer. Perhaps, now, those who control the distribution of sponsorship and television revenue will be more aware of the parlous position of many county players. In 1977 Schweppes sponsored the county championship, and for their money received daily publicity in every national newspaper. Unfortunately the sponsorship came at a time of governmental pay restrictions and initially their support, although welcome to the county clubs, has made no appreciable difference to the pay packets of individual cricketers.

The system has lacked incentive in two ways. There has been less and less reason for the promising schoolboy to choose a career in the game to the exclusion of a more certain future in business. Moreover, for those in the profession there has been no real inducement, short of ambition and pride, to reach the top. For all the additional pressure and hard work, the extra rewards have been measured in hundreds rather than thousands of pounds.

It was really this outdated system which brought me into county cricket. Overseas players were welcomed because the game had stagnated; young athletes in the country were turning to football or other pursuits. The county game was full of old men. For all the exceptions, like Bill Alley who made 3,000 runs in the 1961 season for Somerset at the age of forty-two, and Ray Illingworth, who in his forties has at last established a need for a trophy cabinet in the Leicester pavilion, players should not need, or be encouraged, to remain in the game until such advanced ages.

You can never be as good at thirty-five as you are at twenty-five, and I believe that if players want to continue in the game they should be paid proportionately less past that point. Then many who otherwise would have hung on will go out of the game, creating greater opportunities for the young blood. At the moment every county has guys who are staying on the staff, even though they are not the players they were five years earlier, and they are drawing the salaries that should be invested in youth.

Since I am a South African, fewer fingers have been pointed at me for my choosing life in the 'circus'. Short of the joking greeting of 'Hello pirate!' most of my team-mates at Southampton understood my thinking and after all, until the question of the ban was raised, Hampshire remained unaffected. The Packer argument remains one of ethics, but for some reason those who speak out most ethically are those who seem to resent cricketers earning good money. 'We pay labourers' wages to labourers' is a remark I have heard from one first-class county. Yet no one complains when Johnny Miller collects 80,000 dollars for two appearances on the golf circuit in Australia, or when Duncan McKenzie moves from Leeds United to Anderlecht and back to Everton with enormous wages and shares of transfer fees which have built up what he calls his 'pot of gold'. Whether you think it selfish or not, the rebels do have a cause.

Many followers of the game could not understand Bob Woolmer's allegiance to the Packer circus—particularly as it came after his Test hundreds against Australia in 1977 had really established him in the England side. Bob's reasoning was simple and very understandable. Though the rewards for Test match appearances had been made much greater there was no certainty that he would keep his place over the years; loss of form or injury could put him on the sidelines and drastically cut down his earnings. The Packer contract offered a *guarantee* of a high salary over a number of years.

As soon as I knew that newspapers all over the globe were going to press with reports of the Packer enterprise emblazoned across their front pages, my first reaction was to call Brian Rakich, the secretary of the Midland-Guildford club in Perth. Because I had been sworn to secrecy I had been able to do no more than hedge in response to the offer of a second year's contract with the club. That first year had been such an enjoyable experience that I wanted to tell Brian that I had thrown in my lot with Packer before he read about it in the papers. I owed the club that much because I could have been treated no better by their organisation. Just as in my previous year in Adelaide, I forged much stronger friendships than one would normally do over a five- or six-month period. But for Packer I would undoubtedly have returned for another season rather than go back to South Africa.

Even before I had picked up a bat for my new club I was in their debt. They managed to suppress a news story which had been headlines of the wrong sort at home. Shelley and I flew from London to South Africa for two weeks before setting off for Perth. But her husband—the marriage had been all but over when we met—had given his story to the popular press. As we disembarked at Johannesburg airport we were surrounded by journalists. What followed were perhaps the worst two weeks of my life. One *Daily News* reporter, who had been a personal friend, would ring up pretending to be someone else in an attempt to scoop the story; another reporter 'borrowed' a pass key to my flat and just walked in on Sunday morning at eight o'clock; the phone never stopped ringing. Yet months earlier, Shelley's husband, a well-known rugby player in Australia, had privately sorted out the problem with me—or so I thought. Fortunately a lawyer friend of Norman Featherstone came to my rescue, and what should always have been a private matter was finally settled privately.

Once again my already tarnished reputation in my own country was given another coating of grime. Perhaps that explains why none of my exploits with Midland received a single line of coverage at home, even though I was the top scorer in Western Australian grade cricket. Perhaps it was because I played no first-class cricket but then neither did Geoff Boycott, and though his connections with South Africa are slightly more tenuous than mine, his run-scoring, also at grade level with Waverley, was well documented.

Again I felt hurt at the lack of interest—another reminder that one or two moments of controversy had wiped out the memories of the years I played for Natal hoping that I was doing my bit to bring about a return to international cricket. Even when one journalist did track me down by telephone in Perth, his treatment of the story cast me in a villainous role once more. This, the only call I received in six months, concerned Peter Kirsten, who had rattled up century after century in the Currie Cup, five in successive innings. What, I was asked, did I think of Kirsten and his achievement? What achievement? I replied. The Perth papers carried no Currie Cup reports. After the explanation, I made the usual admiring noises about a record which was, after all, deserving of praise. But the sub-editor who put the article into the paper could only pick out one hardly relevant fact: that the Australian papers had not mentioned the feat. The headline over the piece read 'Australians don't want to know Kirsten'.

No wonder I found Perth such a haven in the storm. As in Adelaide, the club organised my stay with a skilled touch, far better than their professional counterparts in England; Hampshire, I've always felt, took an insufficient interest in my accommodation problems when I first arrived. Under the guidance of Alf Charleson, the president, the Barry Richards Project was established and, through the efforts of a large number of members, the costs of my visit were totally covered by sponsorship. I would spend the weekdays coaching for sponsors, such as the Perth Building

Society, for whom I went to the nets with Tony Lock; at weekends we played the matches.

Life offered a variety that I had rarely found in England or South Africa. Bob Meuleman, who had nearly caught me on the brink of my three hundred, owned a squash centre, where almost every day he would delight in giving me a five-point start and then wiping the court with me. Whenever there was first-class cricket in Perth, apart from Saturday afternoons when I was playing, I would comment on the match for the local television station or newspaper. At the big matches against the Pakistanis and the MCC I did the television commentary with Richie Benaud and Ian Chappell, again sensing that I would enjoy following in Richie's footsteps. I even did a television commercial for a range of cars, driving up to the camera and uttering the selling lines.

At thirty-one I was the old man of the Midland team, with the majority in their mid-twenties, while the baby was Mark O'Neill, the seventeen-year-old son of Norman. Because I was supposed to be the cure for their slump the previous season, when they had dropped to the bottom reaches of the table, I felt under pressure, but their sheer enthusiasm revitalised me. I took them training, and to my surprise wanted to join in, so that I regained that level of fitness I had lost several years earlier.

One fixture took us to the famous goldmining town of Kalgoorlie, about two hundred and fifty miles east of Perth. On a baking afternoon, the sun so hot it would wrinkle your skin like a prune, I was finding it difficult to accumulate runs at the normal rapid pace required in the limited time of the grade game; their bowlers' predilection for firing three or four deliveries an over way down the leg side didn't exactly help. Eventually one rather large spectator on the cover boundary, who had been making sure that his inside was not as warm as his outside by, in true Aussie fashion, swilling cans of cold beer, lost patience with me. 'Richards,' he yelled, 'I'll give you fifty dollars if you hit the next ball for four.'

Much as expected, the next delivery started outside the leg stump but with some brisk footwork I managed to get inside it. Third bounce, the ball disappeared into the crowd not five yards from where the heckler was sitting. Sure enough, when I got out, the gentleman strode across to intercept my exit and pulled out a fifty-dollar note. I settled, instead, for a much more welcome can of beer.

Though I started tentatively, I scored consistently for the club, and I was very glad to be able to repay their kindness by helping them win the minor premiership with the most points from the grade games. But in their system this only earned a place in a play-off of the top four. Both semi-finals were staged simultaneously on the Western Australian ground in Perth, which is so vast that with only a slight overlap of boundary two playing areas can be used. In our semi-final Midland took on the University club, and I hit my best form of the summer.

At tea I was 20 not out, and Keith Slater, who as a Midland committee man had played such a big part in bringing me to the club, took the opportunity to nip away from the match for a quick business call. When he returned an hour later, he noticed that I was out and assumed that the last man figure, which read 127, was a mistake and should have been 27. In fact in not much more than three-quarters of an hour I had slogged a hundred, including one of the two best shots I have ever played in my life. Against a leg-spin bowler, I went on to the back foot and hit a six, which must have carried over eighty yards, straight over cover's head.

The best compliment I received for it came from Trevor Chappell, who was playing in the other semi-final on the adjoining pitch. He made a point of coming over and congratulating me, which is remarkable because it is very rare that any of the Chappells show great enthusiasm for that sort of thing; they are all very hard to please. Perhaps as a reaction, Rod Marsh, who was also playing—for Scarborough—in the other match, smashed 50 in seventeen minutes.

By coincidence, the other shot I really treasure was also played at Perth. When Western Australia took the second new ball during my triple century in 1970, I hit Dennis Lillee back over his head; the ball crashed against the top of the sight screen and ricocheted back into the playing area.

Scarborough in fact beat us in the final when their greater experience, with seven players who had represented the state, was just too much for us. In my last innings for Midland I reached 43 in quick time but then flicked at one and was caught. I subsequently found out that I was one run short of the club record for a season. Though you've read my views on statistics, I would have enjoyed that landmark; after throwing my wicket away so often it was quite galling to come so close. Now I share the record, 898 runs, with Kevin Gartrell, who had reached that total eight years earlier and was still a valuable member of the side.

One of the highlights of the summer was a trip to the Centenary Test in Melbourne. Craig Serjeant and I were tour leaders for a party of cricket-lovers from the area, and just being there brought back so much of my childhood love for the game which more recent experience had eaten away. Just about everybody from the world of cricket was present; from breakfast to closedown the media devoted their total attention to the great event. Even though I had to fly back in the middle to carry on a grade innings —I was 140 not out against Subiaco from the previous weekend— I was a wide-eyed fan again for a few days, watching a match so remarkable that you would almost believe that it had been scripted. England's tremendous early bowling which was set back by their flimsy batting, Australia's mammoth second innings which was almost beaten by Derek Randall's 174, and then the final margin of victory for Australia by 45 runs—an exact replica of the result of the very first Test match between the two countries. Sharing, if only as a spectator, in moments such as those made personal disappointments seem trivial.

Shortly after that I had to return to England, earlier than usual because although the season had not yet been complicated by the revelation of the Packer episode, I had to step straight into the running of my benefit. The cheese and wine party that I held at Dennis Tobin's house was hardly adequate return for all the endeavour spent on my behalf, but it provided a rowdy, if somewhat nostalgic, finish to an experiment that for me had been an unqualified success.

I can hardly say the same about my benefit season, this strange system of reward for loyal service where a player, usually ten years after he is capped, is given an opportunity by his county to receive donations from the public, like a charity. The off-the-field distractions disrupted my form. Hampshire is not an easy county in which to enlist support, along with Derbyshire, Gloucestershire and perhaps Somerset. On the other hand the cricket fanaticism in Kent, Warwickshire and Lancashire is so strong that beneficiaries in those counties simply fall into the groove of the previous year and reap the rewards.

At Hampshire the small enthusiastic bunch of volunteers who run the supporters' club have enough problems sustaining their enterprise. Apart from one or two major events—for example the focal point of my benefit was a pro-celebrity golf match, which was turned into a real success by the kind support of Gary Player —there is a responsibility for the beneficiary to travel the county to meet his supporters.

I have never been a man for the four-ale bar, and, although I met many very pleasant and generous people in my travels, I always stepped into my car for an evening's tour of the hostelries with a heavy heart. For every four pleasant calls there would always be one at which hostility rather than hospitality was the prevailing atmosphere. There you are insulted over your last innings—they never remember the previous years—or you are taken on by those who work in factories or on building sites and can't understand why you should get a benefit when they have no such advantage to support their family.

Various local clubs staged matches in order to make a donation to my benefit fund and I was fortunate that certain clubs made splendid efforts in this respect, though the wetness of the summer proved to be a handicap. I didn't feel that I had all the help I might have expected from my team-mates in playing in those games which weren't washed out. For a pro who desperately wants a day's rest from the game, such occasions are as welcome as a letter from the taxman, but usually they will turn out; one day, you see, they will have a benefit of their own and they will need your presence.

My situation was different: once the likelihood of my being banned because of Packer became apparent, the support fell away, and was never helped by a succession of injuries to first-team players. On one occasion when the Hampshire Hogs club really went out of their way to create a superb day, I was the only capped player in my select side and I shouldn't have played because I was injured. At other times friends from other counties came to my rescue; Geoff Howarth from Surrey drove eighty miles from London to play in a game one Friday night; Chris Waller from Sussex and Tim Lamb from Middlesex were others to whom I had cause to be grateful. Without the willingness of the Hampshire 2nd XI I would have had to take on certain matches almost single-handed.

As it turned out, despite all the heartaches at the time, the benefit was a great success, and I do want to thank all the Hampshire folk who really did me proud. I only wish I could have expressed my gratitude with a record number of runs during the season.

However, my involvement with my benefit, together with one or two niggling injuries, which caused me to miss a number of matches, upset the harmony of the dressing-room. What had begun as a difference of opinion with one regular member of the side became a direct clash of personalities; others, less antipathetic, became increasingly fed-up with my general discontent. Because I was not playing to my full capabilities I deserved some of their criticism, but I would still point out that I averaged 42 for the season, and that I played my part in our run to the semi-finals of the Benson & Hedges Cup.

In that match I was the first victim in a Prockie hat-trick which tilted the match towards Gloucestershire. A highly respected and senior umpire adjudged me lbw, though I felt sure I had edged the ball on to my pad—an occupational hazard which every batsman has to come to terms with. It wasn't a good week for me with umpires. Four days earlier at Worcester I nicked a delivery to second slip and didn't walk: I had jammed down on the ball as it reached me almost on the full and I simply had no idea where it had gone. When I saw it in the fielder's hands I didn't have a clue how it got there. So I waited for the umpire's decision, even though it probably looked blatantly out to everyone else on the ground.

The dressing-room disharmony reached its lowest point at the end of the season at Scarborough. The Fenner Trophy, a one-day competition between four counties, and a three-day game against T. N. Pearce's XI for the entertainment of holiday crowds, hardly constitute the ultimate in competition. At the end of my season it was the last thing I needed, and I begged Richard Gilliat to excuse me. It seemed to me an ideal opportunity for one of the county's promising young players, for whom the appearance money would be a real bonus. But I was selected for the festival because the selection committee felt duty bound to provide the organisers, the large holiday crowd and the sponsors with a full-strength Hampshire team. In fact I was dropped for the Fenner Trophy final because Richard was unhappy with my approach to the semi-final, and thought it would be in everyone's interests that I should be twelfth man—a role I thoroughly enjoyed.

Because we were at Scarborough, the Hampshire players were unable to attend the extraordinary meeting called by the Cricketers' Association, the players' union, to discuss whether to support or reject the TCCB's call for the ban on Packer players. Instead we recorded a postal vote; the result was 16 votes in support of the ban and only 1 against it. When you consider we had three players, Greenidge, Roberts and myself, who were directly affected, those figures might surprise you. Gordon, in fact, was the only player who wanted a retraction so that we could play county cricket again.

That letter was posted to Jack Bannister, the secretary of the Association, on Friday September 2nd with the meeting scheduled for the afternoon of Monday 5th. On the Sunday I met Tony Greig at a Packer get-together and told him how I had voted. He wasn't pleased because he felt I had let down those 'pirates' who would still like to continue playing in the championship; Prockie and Eddie Barlow were among those to whom a ban would mean great disappointment. Though I couldn't bring myself to share their point of view, I did not want to let them down.

At eleven o'clock on the morning of the meeting I rang Edgbaston, where the players from all the counties were congregating, and asked to speak to David Brown, who is chairman of the Cricketers' Association. He wasn't there so I left a message to the effect that instead of voting for the ban, I wished to abstain on all motions connected with the Packer business. But David Brown was never informed of my call.

In fact the regulations of the debating process did not include provision for postal votes and none of the Hampshire votes were included in the final figures; these showed a small majority in favour of the ban. Yet the Hampshire letter was read out to the meeting, and caused great amusement; it did not take much deduction from those who were well acquainted with my disillusionment with county cricket that Gordon had been the solitary voice to challenge the motion. It appeared that I had let Greiggy down, and especially Prockie and Barlow. When I heard that my phone call had not been acted on, I was furious.

I was told about the meeting at Bristol, where we had travelled from Scarborough; for what might yet prove to be my final taste of county cricket on the ground where it had all begun with Gloucestershire 2nd XI more than twelve years previously. Nor was it the scene of any end-of-season irrelevance: a win for Prockie, now captain of the county, would bring them the county championship for the first time in a hundred years. But it was no occasion for friendly feelings to infiltrate our own desire to win, with the spotlight back on us again after a season spent mostly in the shadows or in the shelter from the ever-present rain.

In the first innings Gordon and I shared a big opening partnership which helped Hampshire to a first-innings lead. Then Gordon crashed 94 when Prockie set his declaration, and his charge eventually brought us home by 4 wickets. Instead of Gloucestershire, Middlesex and Kent shared the title. At the start of the final day's play, to my own surprise, the rest of our team encircled Gordon and myself out in the middle and sang 'Auld Lang Syne', expecting that the ban would prevent our return. I would like to think that the feelings which inspired the gesture were sincere; at the time I was sure that they were enjoying a huge joke. I hope I was wrong.

Epilogue

As I write, prior to leaving for Australia to join Kerry Packer, it still remains to be seen how appropriate was that singing of Auld Lang Syne. Because of this uncertainty I left England with very mixed feelings. Elsewhere in the book I have clearly spelt out my discontent with the demands made on county cricketers day in day out. On dismal May mornings in front of a couple of hundred spectators on an away ground, I have wanted the cricket world to stop so that I could get off. But then the decision to leave county cricket rested solely with me.

Though the enforcement of the ban will certainly put an end to those dreary hours when I have had to delve deep into my resources of professionalism to maintain the necessary level of concentration, the possibility of being forced out of the English game has made me reflect on some of the many enjoyable moments I have experienced.

Should I not be allowed to play for Hampshire again I shall miss the confrontations with great bowlers. People often ask me what it's like to face Dennis Lillee or Jeff Thomson, Michael Holding or Wayne Daniel, and I suppose one of the most dramatic phases of first-class cricket is the opening batsmen taking guard against a real speed merchant with the new ball. But as an opening batsman this has been my job—a test of my technique and reflexes against swing, movement off the seam and, of course, sheer pace.

The greater challenges for me, probably because they occur less frequently, have been taking on the very best spin bowlers. I have written earlier of the crucial match in our championship season when we beat Northamptonshire at Southampton, when Northants were really pressing us at the top of the table. Although we needed only 90 to win in the fourth innings the wicket had developed into a real turner, just what we didn't want because of the presence of Bishen Bedi in their side.

This was no occasion for the death or glory innings; there was too much at stake. Throughout my career I have always carried the fight to spinners, and that philosophy has by and large served me well. But against Bedi on a wicket that was helping him, I couldn't take the risk. Some spinners get over-excited when conditions are in their favour; instead of letting the wicket work for them they lose their length in direction. But not Bishen.

His great talent is that he bowls with the same action all the time but produces an immense variety. One delivery might be pushed through quickly, while the next would take a loopier trajectory and have you playing too soon. Then he bowls one which floats in to the right-hander. He'll try to tempt you with a wider delivery. On top of those variations he subtly mixes up the amount of spin. He is a genuine finger-spinner who can make the ball deviate even on good wickets, but once he senses a batsman is playing for the turn he rolls his fingers over the ball rather than twisting it out of his hand and that delivery just goes on with the arm. I've seen him pick up lots of wickets in this way, often through catches at silly-point with the ball striking the pad first of all and then the bat.

When cricket is talked of as an art it is these types of skill that come to my mind. That day at Southampton in 1973 I knew I was watching an artist at work and I was proud to survive that challenge. We had plenty of time to make the runs so I settled for the cagey approach—a case of sitting it out at the crease and waiting for the bad balls. Bishen doesn't bowl many of those, so it was a long wait; meanwhile every delivery had to be watched right on to the middle of the bat, though as I remember there were several which thoroughly beat me.

Ray Illingworth is another magnificent spin bowler whom I have always held in great regard. I've lost count of the number of duels we have had in all types of cricket, because, make no mistake, he is one of that rare breed of spinners who can go about their business just as effectively in one-day cricket. With Illy it's that old Yorkshire upbringing again, I'm sure, which makes him such a grudging bowler. Don't get me wrong, I don't mean that he fires it in at medium pace in a defensive style. His control is so good that he is both economical and attacking, though I have felt that towards the twilight of his career he didn't bowl enough. Nevertheless Leicestershire more than paid their dues to the spinners union, with Jackie Birkenshaw, Chris Balderstone, John Steele and Illy bowling more slow stuff than most county attacks. I can only commend the Yorkshire committee for taking the bold step of making Ray Illingworth their team manager when he retires; his is too good a cricketing brain to be lost to the game.

No discussion of spin and county cricket can finish without a mention of Derek Underwood—known as 'Deadly' to every professional because of his ability to bowl sides out when he gets going on a bad wicket. Even on a good wicket he is an awk-ward bowler to attack because of his extra pace through the air. But on a good track he is much less likely to tease you out than a Bedi or an Illingworth. Yet his record is tremendous and there aren't that many bad wickets in a season. His Test career, of course, is now in jeopardy because of his decision to play for Kerry Packer, but had it continued uninterrupted he would have been an absolute certainty to break Lance Gibbs's record of the most Test wickets. Perhaps on a good wicket 'great' is a slight over-statement of his talent, but on a wet turner he is more than 'great'; he is the unplayable bowler.

Funnily enough, sheer speed has never been a shattering prob-lem for me, though any batsman who tells you he really enjoys blistering pace is not telling the truth. The three times I have been hit on the head have all been because of miscalculations on my part, and though I have had my embarrassing moments against the quickies—I recall Bob Willis once leaving me in an undignified posture having brushed my cap to the ground with a bouncer—I have not felt especially vulnerable.

Where I am more likely to get out is against medium-pacers. Robin Jackman, that effervescent character, has probably dis-missed me more times than any other bowler, but he has played against me the whole year round for several seasons now—for Surrey against Hampshire and for Rhodesia against Natal. He falls into a category of seamers who bowl a good line at the off stump at a pace that is brisk, but not brisk enough to stop me wanting to smash them through the offside for four.

The very best of this type are Geoff Arnold, who would have played more for England but for a succession of injuries, and Mike Hendrick who has taken over Arnold's mantle in international cricket. Both are great bowlers because they have mastery of that deadly delivery with the new ball, the out swinger. More than that every so often one will hit the seam and nip back into the right-hander who is usually overcompensating for the away swing by shuffling across his stumps. Take a look in the papers or in a back copy of Wisden and you'll see a lot of dismissals 'lbw bowled Arnold' and 'lbw bowled Hendrick, with that "nip-backer" '—as well as the many victims caught behind the wicket or in the slips that the outswinger brings them.

Both Geoff and Mike know that I am unable to resist playing my shots outside the off stump; against them the odds are that I shall give the slips catching practice. So I try to make them bowl at me rather than blaze away at the tempting wide deliveries that swing wider that they usually greet me with. Again, it's a case of resisting temptation. Six outswingers that start outside the off-stump and then swing untouched through to the keeper's gloves are a wasted over, especially with the new ball. If I manage to achieve that degree of patience, the bowler is forced to bowl at the stumps to make me play a shot; then I have the chance to attack with less risk—unless of course I miss a straight one.

In 1977 Mike Hendrick bowled to me at Chesterfield and I don't think any batsman in the world could have made runs against him that day. He raced through Hampshire finishing with figures of about 6 for 30 and in doing so he was desperately unlucky. A true reflection of skill would have been 10 for 15; it was a brilliant spell of bowling, and if he can stay fit—like Arnold his career has been disrupted with pulls and strains—he will be a great asset to England in the future.

As for the batsmen I admire, thankfully I shall still have the opportunity of watching Greg Chappell at close-quarters in the 'super-tests'. When I played against him during his two years with Somerset he was still developing, as he was when we were team-mates for South Australia. But for the past five years or so he has been one of the few great batsmen in the contemporary game. For me his real strength is in his ability to play completely straight; much of the run-getting in cricket today is a combination of nicks and nudges. The game is full of players who 'work' the ball on the leg-side by playing across the line. Greg accumulates runs through mid-wicket as well as anyone but he does it with the full swing of the bat. If I was offered a lift in a car to drive a couple of hundred miles with the assurance of seeing Greg Chappell bat at the end of the journey I'd be off like a shot.

My namesake, Vivian, from Antigua, is less of a stylist but undoubtedly a player of the very highest class. Like all West Indians he has days when he seems to cast away his wicket, attempting the flamboyant, but unlike all but the best he is capable of playing innings of great quantity and quality. His vintage year of 1976 when he collected 1,710 runs in Test cricket set a new high at that level but if the structure of the game remains unaltered he is well-equipped to set new targets.

Lest I should be accused of a bias in favour of overseas cricketers in the English game, I would also place John Edrich on my list of great players. Those who regard him as a dour grafter would do well to remember that in the early sixties his style was to set about the county attacks; he had a spell when he hit more sixes than any other player in the country. But when he was entrusted with the job of stabilising the England batting line-up, often in sides that were under the collar against the Australian and West Indian pace attacks, he set about the task with maximum efficiency and responsibility. Don't forget either that although he limited his strokes to get the innings off to a sound start he would still hit the ball very hard later in his innings when the pressure was off. By nature Australians are far from generous with their praise but their top players all have the profoundest respect for the record of John Edrich over the past twenty years and it's a respect that I share.

When I came to England as a county player in 1968, John Edrich was starting out on the latter phase of his career. He'll still be playing county cricket in 1978, and it may be that I will not. The final paragraphs of an autobiography should really sum up the end of a period in one's life and make firm predictions about the future. After several years of stable, if not altogether comfortable, routine I have clear memories only of the distant past. The present and the future are a jumble of possibilities.

Of cricket there seems to be nothing but acceptance of my label as a Text exile. I have learned to live with that disappointment but I hope that the international arena provided by Kerry Packer will make up for some of the big occasions I have missed. For all my inner misgivings about those wickets which have been cultivated in greenhouses and then planted out in the middle, I am really looking forward to the 'super-tests' and I have trained hard to get back into the peak of condition.

From there my future still rests on the decisions of the courts. I am under contract to play for Hampshire until the end of the 1979 season, but the TCCB may not allow me to fulfil it. Thanks to my benefit I am now financially secure even without a Test career, and as you may have gathered through the preceding pages insecurity has always been a source of worry to me. Now the choice of whether finally to settle in England, Australia or back home in South Africa becomes that much simpler.

If the politics of cricket have been unkind to those ambitions I cherished ten years ago, I am full of gratitude to the game for what it has brought me and I like to think I have contributed to its benefit in return. Though I cannot put my hand on my heart and say that I would not change anything that has happened in my life—no South African who has lost a Test career could do that with honesty—it never stops me counting my blessings.

Appendix

B. A. RICHARDS (SOUTH AFRICA, NATAL, HAMPSHIRE
AND SOUTH AUSTRALIA) CAREER ANALYSIS
compiled by
VICTOR H. ISAACS & PETER A. SICHEL

Season	Country	Matches	Innings	Not out	Runs	Highest innings	Average	100	50	Catches
1964–65	In South Africa	5	7	0	156	63	22·28	0	1	2
1965	In England	1	1	0	59	59	59·00	0	1	0
1965–66	In South Africa	7	11	1	427	77	42·70	0	5	3
1966–67	In South Africa	7	12	1	553	107	50·27	1	5	6
1967–68	In South Africa	6	11	1	675	146	67·50	4	1	3
1968	In England	33	55	5	2,395	206	47·90	5	18	37
1968–69	In South Africa	8	15	2	763	112*	58·69	1	7	5
1969	In England	20	31	6	1,440	155	57·60	5	5	17
1969–70	In South Africa	10	18	2	1,172	169	73·25	6	3	9
1970	In England	20	33	2	1,667	153	53·77	3	12	15
1970–71	In Australia	10	16	2	1,538	356	109·85	6	3	10
1971	In South Africa	1	2	0	207	140	103·50	1	1	0
1971	In England	24	45	4	1,938	141*	47·26	2	17	33
1971–72	In South Africa	8	15	1	1,089	219	77·78	4	4	4
1972	In England	19	33	1	1,425	118	44·53	4	8	28
1972–73	In South Africa	10	19	1	1,247	197	69·27	5	5	9
1973	In England	18	30	2	1,452	240	51·85	5	4	35
1973–74	In South Africa	12	18	2	1,285	186*	80·31	4	8	12
1974	In England	19	27	4	1,406	225*	61·13	4	6	23
1974–75	In South Africa	11	21	2	891	162	46·89	4	3	9
1975	In England	19	32	5	1,621	135*	60·03	3	13	22
1975–76	In South Africa	11	21	4	1,051	159	61·82	3	5	12
1976	In England	18	34	2	1,572	179	49·12	7	3	32
1977	In England	16	25	3	927	115	42·13	2	5	19
		313	532	53	26,956	356	56·27	79	143	345

IN ENGLAND

Season	Matches	Innings	Not out	Runs	Highest innings	Average	100	50	Catches
1965	1	1	0	59	59	59·00	0	1	0
1968	33	55	5	2,395	206	47·90	5	18	37

Season	Matches	Innings	Not out	Runs	Highest innings	Average	100	50	Catches
1969	20	31	6	1,440	155	57·60	5	5	17
1970	20	33	2	1,667	153	53·77	3	12	15
1971	24	45	4	1,938	141*	47·26	2	17	33
1972	19	33	1	1,425	118	44·53	4	8	28
1973	18	30	2	1,452	240	51·85	5	4	35
1974	19	27	4	1,406	225*	61·13	4	6	23
1975	19	32	5	1,621	135*	60·03	3	13	22
1976	18	34	2	1,572	179	49·12	7	3	32
1977	16	25	3	927	115	42·13	2	5	19
	207	346	34	15,902	240	50·96	40	92	261

IN SOUTH AFRICA

Season	Matches	Innings	Not out	Runs	Highest innings	Average	100	50	Catches
1964–65	5	7	0	156	63	22·28	0	1	2
1965–66	7	11	1	427	77	42·70	0	5	3
1966–67	7	12	1	553	107	50·27	1	5	6
1967–68	6	11	1	675	146	67·50	4	1	3
1968–69	8	15	2	763	112*	58·69	1	7	5
1969–70	10	18	2	1,172	169	73·25	6	3	9
1971	1	2	0	207	140	103·50	1	1	0
1971–72	8	15	1	1,089	219	77·78	4	4	4
1972–73	10	19	1	1,247	197	69·27	5	5	9
1973–74	12	18	2	1,285	186*	80·31	4	8	12
1974–75	11	21	2	891	162	46·89	4	3	9
1975–76	11	21	4	1,051	159	61·82	3	5	12
	96	170	17	9,516	219	62·19	33	48	74

IN AUSTRALIA

Season	Matches	Innings	Not out	Runs	Highest innings	Average	100	50	Catches
1970–71	10	16	2	1,538	356	109·85	6	3	10
GRAND TOTAL	313	532	53	25,956	356	56·27	79	143	345

	Innings	Not out	Runs	Highest innings	Average	100	50
AGAINST SIDES IN ENGLAND							
An England XI	8	1	257	64	36·71	0	1
Australian Touring Team	6	1	328	96	65·60	0	4
Indian Touring Team	3	0	104	49	34·66	0	0
MCC	1	0	189	189	189·00	1	0
New Zealand Touring Team	4	0	345	132	86·25	2	1
Pakistan Touring Team	4	1	231	100	77·00	1	1
Rest of the World XI	2	0	74	68	37·00	0	1
South African Touring Team	1	0	59	59	59·00	0	1
West Indian Touring Team	2	1	206	120*	206·00	1	1
Oxford University	4	0	354	133	88·50	1	3
Derbyshire	13	0	473	153	36·38	2	2
Essex	15	1	704	176	50·28	2	3
Glamorgan	21	3	869	111	48·27	2	6
Gloucestershire	29	2	1,056	94	39·11	0	8
Kent	32	4	1,515	179	54·10	6	4
Lancashire	16	1	717	155	47·80	3	2
Leicestershire	17	2	930	150	62·00	3	5
Middlesex	18	3	762	86	50·80	0	8
Northamptonshire	19	6	1,056	130	81·23	3	7
Nottinghamshire	14	1	824	225*	63·38	3	2
Somerset	23	1	804	81	36·54	0	8
Surrey	22	2	872	120	43·60	2	5
Sussex	26	2	1,000	136	41·66	3	5
Warwickshire	17	0	1,016	240	59·76	4	5
Worcestershire	16	1	748	103	49·86	1	6
Yorkshire	13	1	409	82	34·08	0	3
	346	34	15,902	240	50·96	40	92
AGAINST SIDES IN SOUTH AFRICA							
Australian Touring Team	6	1	385	107	77·00	1	3
Australia (Test Matches)	7	0	508	140	72·57	2	2
Eastern Province	35	3	2,029	152	63·40	8	11
Festival XI	2	0	207	140	103·50	1	1
International Wanderers	4	0	165	80	41·25	0	2
MCC	6	0	145	63	24·16	0	1
North XI	1	0	0	0	0·00	0	0
North Eastern Transvaal	3	1	155	123	77·50	1	0
Rhodesia	28	4	1,946	219	81·08	7	8
D. H. Robins' XI	15	2	704	180	54·15	2	3
Transvaal	36	2	1,809	146	53·20	7	9
Western Province	25	3	1,413	186*	64·22	4	8
	170	17	9,516	219	62·19	33	48

	Innings	Not out	Runs	Highest innings	Average	100	50
AGAINST SIDES IN AUSTRALIA							
MCC Touring Team	3	0	393	224	131·00	2	0
New South Wales	3	1	265	178	132·50	1	1
Queensland	3	0	203	155	67·66	1	0
Victoria	4	0	270	105	67·50	1	2
Western Australia	3	1	407	356	203·50	1	0
	16	2	1,538	356	109·85	6	3
GRAND TOTAL	532	53	26,956	356	56·27	79	143

For Teams

	Innings	Not out	Runs	Highest innings	Average	100	50
Gloucestershire	1	0	59	59	59·00	0	1
Hampshire	331	33	15,270	240	51·24	38	88
International Wanderers	2	0	178	110	89·00	1	1
Natal	137	16	7,508	219	62·04	26	37
D. H. Robins' XI	4	0	235	102	58·75	2	0
Rest of the World XI	10	1	338	81	37·55	0	2
South XI	1	0	0	0	0·00	0	0
South Africa (Tests)	7	0	508	140	72·57	2	2
South African Colts XI	2	0	76	63	38·00	0	1
South African Games XI	2	0	35	25	17·50	0	0
South African Invitation XI	17	1	1,004	180	62·75	3	7
South Australia	16	2	1,538	356	109·85	6	3
Transvaal Invitation XI	2	0	207	140	103·50	1	1
	532	53	26,956	356	56·27	79	143
CURRIE CUP COMPETITION							
1965–66	10	1	427	77	47·44	0	5
1966–67	6	0	168	96	28·00	0	2
1967–68	11	1	675	146	67·50	4	1
1968–69	11	1	565	112*	56·50	1	5
1969–70	7	1	439	169	73·16	3	0
1971–72	15	1	1,089	219	77·78	4	4
1972–73	16	1	1,064	197	70·93	4	5
1973–74	12	1	898	186*	81·63	3	6
1974–75	15	1	597	162	42·64	3	1
1975–76	15	4	868	159	78·90	3	3
	118	12	6,790	219	64·05	25	32

	Innings	Not out	Runs	Highest innings	Average	100	50
AGAINST TEAMS—CURRIE CUP COMPETITION							
Eastern Province	35	3	2,029	152	63·40	8	11
North Eastern Transvaal	3	1	155	123	77·50	1	0
Rhodesia	25	4	1,760	219	83·80	6	7
Transvaal	32	2	1,596	146	53·20	6	8
Western Province	23	2	1,250	186*	59·52	4	6
	118	12	6,790	219	64·05	25	32
JOHN PLAYER LEAGUE							
1969	13	1	405	85*	33·75	0	3
1970	11	2	592	155*	65·77	3	0
1971	16	1	482	81	32·13	0	4
1972	14	2	643	105	53·58	2	4
1973	12	1	381	61	34·63	0	1
1974	13	0	368	123	28·30	1	1
1975	16	1	689	112	45·93	1	5
1976	16	2	710	101	50·71	1	5
1977	10	1	242	102	26·88	1	1
	121	11	4,512	155*	41·01	9	24

CAREER BOWLING FIGURES

		Overs	Maidens	Runs	Wickets	Average
1964–65	In South Africa	16	5	50	1	50·00
1965–66	In South Africa	56	19	114	3	38·00
1966–67	In South Africa	9	2	29	0	—
1967–68	In South Africa	36	3	107	4	26·75
1968	In England	100	33	264	12	22·00
1968–69	In South Africa	33	4	128	2	64·00
1969	In England	98	28	273	7	39·00
1969–70	In South Africa	23	5	60	2	30·00
1970	In England	39	8	138	3	46·00
1970–71	In Australia	37·4	5	145	5	29·00
1971	In England	66	18	184	2	92·00
1971–72	In South Africa	19	2	54	0	—
1972	In England	46	24	82	3	27·33
1972–73	In South Africa	47	5	177	3	59·00
1973	In England	78	26	193	6	32·16
1973–74	In South Africa	43	17	85	4	21·25
1974	In England	37	13	96	2	48·00
1974–75	In South Africa	18	4	58	3	19·33
1975	In England	75	20	227	5	45·40
1975–76	In South Africa	40	8	129	4	32·25
1976	In England	69	22	192	6	32·00
1977	In England	20	3	93	0	—
		1005·4	274	2878	77	37·37

Centuries—First-Class Matches

1966-67
- 107 South African XI v Australians at East London

1967-68
- 146 Natal v Transvaal at Durban
- 135 Natal v Eastern Province at Port Elizabeth
- 123 Natal v North Eastern Transvaal at Pretoria
- 114 Natal v Transvaal at Johannesburg

1968
- 206 Hampshire v Nottinghamshire at Portsmouth
- 176 Hampshire v Essex at Westcliff
- 133 Hampshire v Warwickshire at Basingstoke
- 130 ⎱ Hampshire v Northamptonshire at Northampton
- 104*⎰

1968-69
- 112* Natal v Rhodesia at Durban

1969
- 155 Hampshire v Lancashire at Manchester
- 132 Hampshire v New Zealanders at Southampton
- 127* Hampshire v Northamptonshire at Bournemouth
- 120* Hampshire v West Indians at Southampton
- 103 Hampshire v Worcestershire at Worcester

1969-70
- 169 Natal v Rhodesia at Durban
- 140 South Africa v Australia at Durban
- 126 South Africa v Australia at Port Elizabeth
- 110* Natal v Eastern Province at Port Elizabeth
- 106 Natal v Rhodesia at Salisbury
- 100 Natal v Western Province at Durban

1970
- 153 Hampshire v Derbyshire at Chesterfield
- 150 Hampshire v Leicestershire at Leicester
- 124 Hampshire v Leicestershire at Southampton

1970-71
- 356 South Australia v Western Australia at Perth
- 224 South Australia v MCC at Adelaide
- 178 South Australia v New South Wales at Sydney
- 155 South Australia v Queensland at Brisbane
- 146 South Australia v MCC at Adelaide
- 105 South Australia v Victoria at Adelaide

1971 (Republic Festival Match)
   140   Transvaal Invitation XI v SA Festival XI at Cape Town

1971
   141* Hampshire v Kent at Southampton
   133   Hampshire v Oxford University at Oxford

1971-72
   219   Natal v Rhodesia at Durban
   169   Natal v Western Province at Cape Town
   134   Natal v Transvaal at Johannesburg
   104   Natal v Eastern Province at Durban

1972
   118   Hampshire v Nottinghamshire at Nottingham
   105   Hampshire v Warwickshire at Portsmouth
   104* Hampshire v Essex at Chelmsford
   101   Hampshire v Kent at Folkstone

1972-73
   197   Natal v Rhodesia at Salisbury
   147* Natal v Eastern Province at Port Elizabeth
   125   Natal v Transvaal at Durban
   104   Natal v Transvaal at Johannesburg
   100   SA Invitation XI v D. H. Robins' XI at Johannesburg

1973
   240   Hampshire v Warwickshire at Coventry
   143* Hampshire v Kent at Southampton
   128   Hampshire v Lancashire at Southport
   116   Hampshire v Surrey at Portsmouth
   102   D. H. Robins' XI v New Zealanders at Eastbourne

1973-74
   186* Natal v Western Province at Pietermaritzburg
   180   SA Invitation XI v D. H. Robins' XI at Durban
   152   Natal v Eastern Province at Durban
   106   Natal v Eastern Province at Port Elizabeth

1974
   225* Hampshire v Nottinghamshire at Nottingham
   189   Hampshire v MCC at Lord's
   104   Hampshire v Glamorgan at Southampton
   100   D. H. Robins' XI v Pakistanis at Eastbourne

1974-75
   162   Natal v Rhodesia at Salisbury
   110   International Wanderers v Transvaal at Johannesburg

107 Natal v Transvaal at Durban
101 Natal v Eastern Province at Port Elizabeth

1975
135* Hampshire v Leicestershire at Leicester
126 Hampshire v Sussex at Hove
103 Hampshire v Lancashire at Liverpool

1975–76
159 Natal v Rhodesia at Bulawayo
140 Natal v Western Province at Durban
138 Natal v Eastern Province at Port Elizabeth

1976
179 Hampshire v Kent at Maidstone
159⎫
108⎭ Hampshire v Kent at Southampton
136 Hampshire v Sussex at Hove
120 Hampshire v Surrey at the Oval
111 Hampshire v Glamorgan at Bournemouth
101 Hampshire v Warwickshire at Bournemouth

1977
115 Hampshire v Derbyshire at Bournemouth
100 Hampshire v Sussex at Southampton

CENTURIES—NOT FIRST-CLASS

1962–63
102 South African School's XI v Western Province at Cape Town
106 South African School's XI v Eton College at Eton, Windsor

1970
155* Hampshire v Yorkshire at Hull (John Player League)
132* Hampshire v Kent at Bournemouth (John Player League)
104 Hampshire v Glamorgan at Southampton (John Player League)

1971–72
119 Natal v South African Country Districts XI at Pietermaritzburg.
110 Natal v North Eastern Transvaal at Pretoria (Gillette Cup)

1972
129 Hampshire v Lancashire at Bournemouth (Gillette Cup)
108 D. H. Robins' XI v Middlesex at Eastbourne
105 Hampshire v Leicestershire at Leicester (John Player League)

103   An Overseas XI v D. H. Robins' XI at Eastbourne

101   Hampshire v Worcestershire at Worcester (John Player League)

1974

129   Hampshire v Gloucestershire at Bristol (Benson & Hedges Cup)

123   Hampshire v Glamorgan at Basingstoke (John Player League)

1974–75

152   Natal v Griqualand West at Kimberley (Gillette Cup)

1975

129   Hampshire v Glamorgan at Southampton (Gillette Cup)

112   Hampshire v Leicestershire at Bournemouth (John Player League)

106*   Hampshire v Yorkshire at Scarborough (Fenner Trophy)

1976

101   Hampshire v Essex at Southampton (John Player League)

1977

102   Hampshire v Middlesex at Lord's (John Player League)

101*   Hampshire v Nottinghamshire at Southampton (Gillette Cup)

MODE OF DISMISSAL

Caught	307
Bowled	114
LBW	42
Run Out	9
Stumped	7
Not Out	48
Retired hurt	5
	532

BOWLERS WHO HAVE DISMISSED RICHARDS ON FIVE OR MORE OCCASIONS

15   R. D. Jackman

11   E. J. Barlow

10   J. N. Shepherd and J. A. Snow

8   D. Mackay-Coghill and A. N. Connolly

7   D. J. Brown, G. D. McKenzie, and M. J. Procter

6   A. Buss, A. Hector, D. L. Underwood and C. E. B. Rice

5   A. S. Brown, J. N. Graham, M. A. Nash, P. M. Pollock, D. J. Shepherd and K. Shuttleworth

Hundred in Each Innings

130 and 104* Hampshire v Northamptonshire at Northampton, 1968
159 and 108   Hampshire v Kent at Southampton, 1976

Hundred and a Fifty in One Match

78 and 135   Natal v Eastern Province at Port Elizabeth, 1967–68
58 and 112* Natal v Rhodesia at Durban, 1968–69
86 and 120* Hampshire v West Indians at Southampton, 1969
81 and 126   South Africa v Australia at Port Elizabeth, 1969–70
106 and 69   Natal v Rhodesia at Salisbury, 1969–70
105 and 72   South Australia v Victoria at Adelaide, 1970–71
140 and 67   Transvaal Invitation XI v SA Festival XI at Cape Town, 1971
63 and 104   Natal v Eastern Province at Durban, 1971–72
54 and 104   Natal v Transvaal at Johannesburg, 1972–73
110 and 68   International Wanderers v Transvaal at Johannesburg, 1974–75
159 and 69* Natal v Rhodesia at Bulawayo, 1975–76

Two Fifties in One Match

67 and 64   Natal v Western Province at Durban, 1965–66
88 and 65   South African XI v Australians at Pietermaritzburg, 1966–67
70 and 74   Hampshire v Oxford University at Oxford, 1968
82* and 83   Hampshire v Sussex at Portsmouth, 1968
82 and 81* Natal v Western Province at Cape Town, 1968–69
94 and 66   Hampshire v Worcestershire at Southampton, 1970
75 and 81   Hampshire v Somerset at Portsmouth, 1970
55 and 82   Hampshire v Middlesex at Lord's, 1971
75 and 60* Hampshire v Northamptonshire at Northampton, 1971
77 and 69   Hampshire v Northamptonshire at Northampton, 1972
78 and 66   Natal v Transvaal at Johannesburg, 1973–74
61 and 80   Natal v Western Province at Cape Town, 1973–74
89 and 55* Hampshire v Leicestershire at Portsmouth, 1974
72 and 94   Hampshire v Essex at Bournemouth, 1975
59 and 71* Hampshire v Middlesex at Southampton, 1975
96 and 69* Hampshire v Australians at Southampton, 1975
52 and 63   Hampshire v Warwickshire at Birmingham, 1977

Carrying Bat Through Innings

127* out of 192 Hampshire v Northamptonshire at Bournemouth, 1969

225* out of 344 Hampshire v Nottinghamshire at Nottingham, 1974
71* out of 179 Hampshire v Middlesex at Southampton, 1975

Hundred Before Lunch
Natal v Rhodesia at Salisbury, 1969–70 (1st morning)
Hampshire v Derbyshire at Chesterfield, 1970 (2nd morning)
Hampshire v Surrey at Portsmouth, 1973 (1st morning)
Hampshire v Kent at Southampton, 1973 (2nd morning)
Hampshire v Nottinghamshire at Nottingham, 1974 (2nd morning)
Hampshire v Sussex at Hove, 1975 (1st morning)
Hampshire v Glamorgan at Bournemouth, 1976 (1st morning)
Hampshire v Sussex at Hove, 1976 (1st morning)
Hampshire v Derbyshire at Bournemouth, 1977 (1st morning)

Three Hundred Runs in One Day
325* (356) South Australia v Western Australia at Perth, 1970–71.
(First day of match—79* at lunch, 216* at tea, and 325* at the close)

Century Partnerships
Barry Richards has shared in 114 hundred partnerships, the best of which are:
225 With E. J. Barlow, Rest of the World v Kent at Canterbury, 1968
207 With R. E. Marshall, Hampshire v Nottinghamshire at Portsmouth, 1968
258 With A. M. Short, Natal v Rhodesia at Durban, 1969–70
201 With C. G. Greenidge, Hampshire v Leicestershire at Southampton, 1970
308 With I. M. Chappell, South Australia v Western Australia at Perth, 1970–71
277 With A. J. Woodcock, South Australia v MCC at Adelaide, 1970–71
235 With I. M. Chappell, South Australia v MCC at Adelaide, 1970–71
233 With C. G. Greenidge, Hampshire v Oxford University at Oxford, 1971
219 With M. B. Madsen, Natal v Rhodesia at Durban, 1971–72
241 With C. G. Greenidge, Hampshire v Kent at Southampton, 1973
207 With C. G. Greenidge, Hampshire v Surrey at Portsmouth, 1973
200 With C. G. Greenidge, Hampshire v Lancashire at Southport, 1973
202 With M. N. S. Taylor, Hampshire v Nottinghamshire at Nottingham, 1974